The
DRAWING
BOOK
FOR
KIDS

365 Daily Things
to Draw: Step by Step

Woo! jr
KiDs activities

Woo! Jr. Kids Activities Founder: Wendy Piersall
Production Coordinator: Cassidy Piersall
Cover Illustration: Michael Koch | Sleeping Troll Studios www.sleepingtroll.com
Interior Illustration: Avinash Saini

Published by:
Wendybird Press
2050 S. Eastwood Dr.
Woodstock IL, 60098
www.wendybirdpress.com

ISBN-13: 978-0997799378
ISBN-10: 0997799374

wendybird
press

HOW to USE THiS BOOK!

All you need is a pencil, eraser,
and a piece of paper!

Follow each drawing diagram step by step:

TiPS:

Draw lightly at first, because you might need to erase some lines as you work.

Add details according to the diagrams, but don't worry about being perfect! Artists frequently make mistakes - they just find ways to make their mistakes look interesting.

Don't worry if your drawings don't turn out the way you want them to. Just keep practicing! Sometimes drawing the same thing just a few times will help.

Once you've finished your drawing in pencil you can trace it with a black fineliner pen and color or paint it to your liking.

You can draw a new item or character every day for 365 days - or use your creativity to combine multiple drawings into an entire scene.

Turn the page for some cool composition ideas!

Put drawings together to create full scenes!

– Underwater Scene –

#14
CraB

#16
Starfish

#18
Stingray

#282
MermaiD

#21
Hammerhead Shark

#23
White Shark

#24
Whale

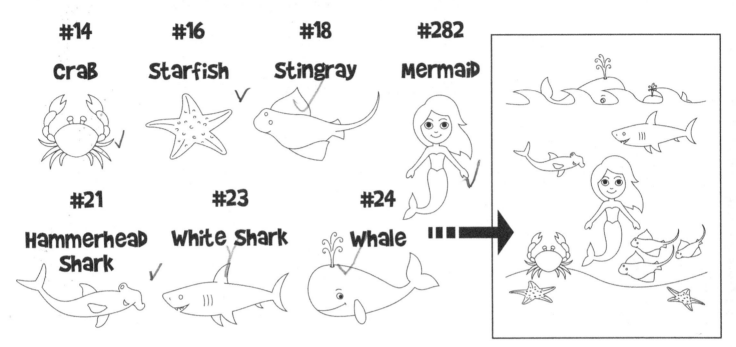

– Fishing Scene –

#29
Fishing Pole

#30
Fish

#79
Waterfall

#292
Boy

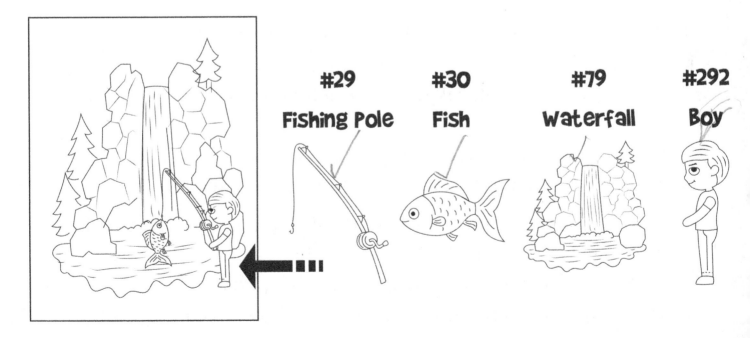

Put Drawings together to create full scenes!

– Outer Space Scene –

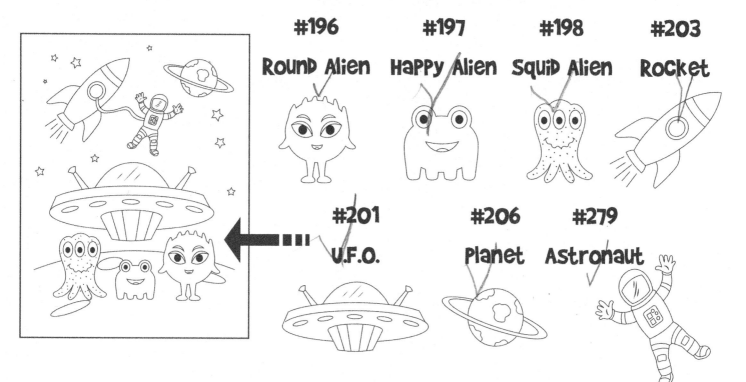

#196 Round Alien
#197 Happy Alien
#198 Squid Alien
#203 Rocket
#201 U.F.O.
#206 Planet
#279 Astronaut

– Flying Fairies Scene –

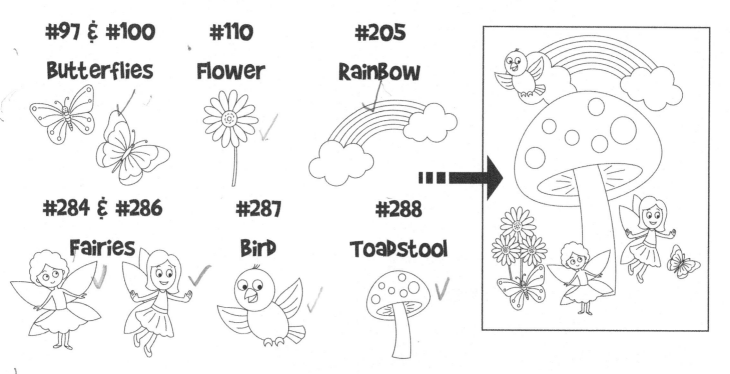

#97 & #100 Butterflies
#110 Flower
#205 Rainbow
#284 & #286 Fairies
#287 Bird
#288 Toadstool

ADD Perspective to your Drawings By using the vanishing Point and a Perspective grid!

The "vanishing point" is a point on the horizon in which a set of parallel lines appear to converge into a single point.
For example, railroad tracks appear to converge in the distance in this photograph:

To use a perspective grid, lightly draw guide lines with a pencil as shown below with a ruler. Then use the grid as a guide for how to angle your lines accurately to convey perspective as shown in the bottom demonstration.

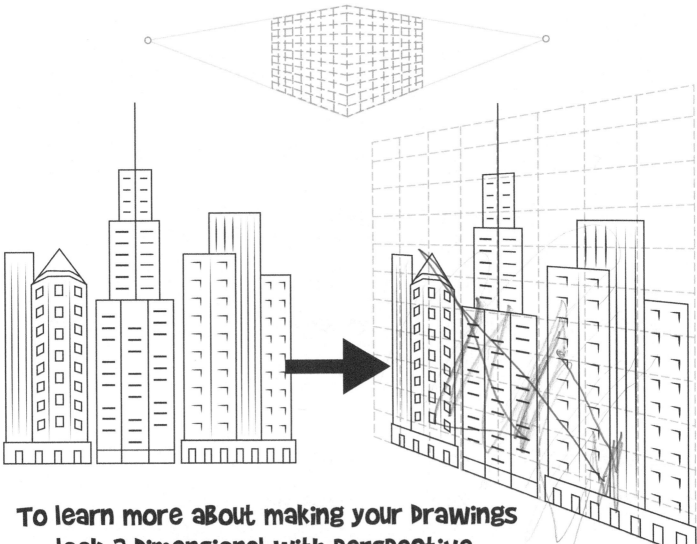

To learn more aBout making your Drawings look 3 Dimensional with Perspective, read our free tutorial at:
www.woojr.com/Perspective

1

2

3

4

5

6

7

8

9

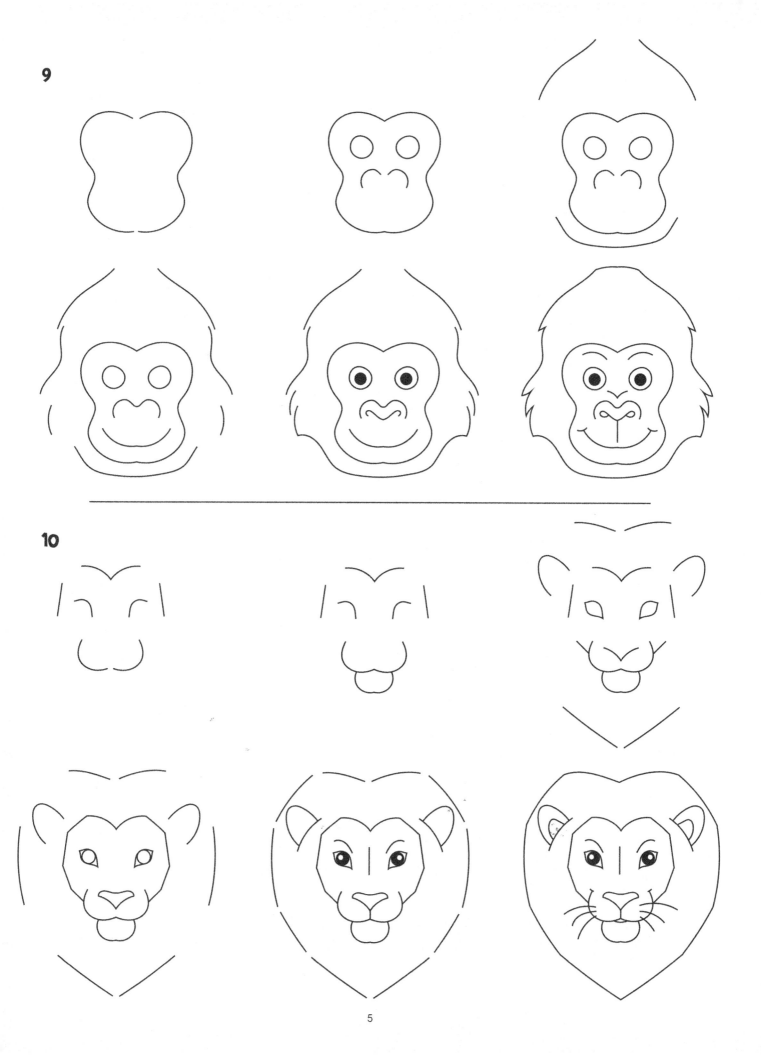

10

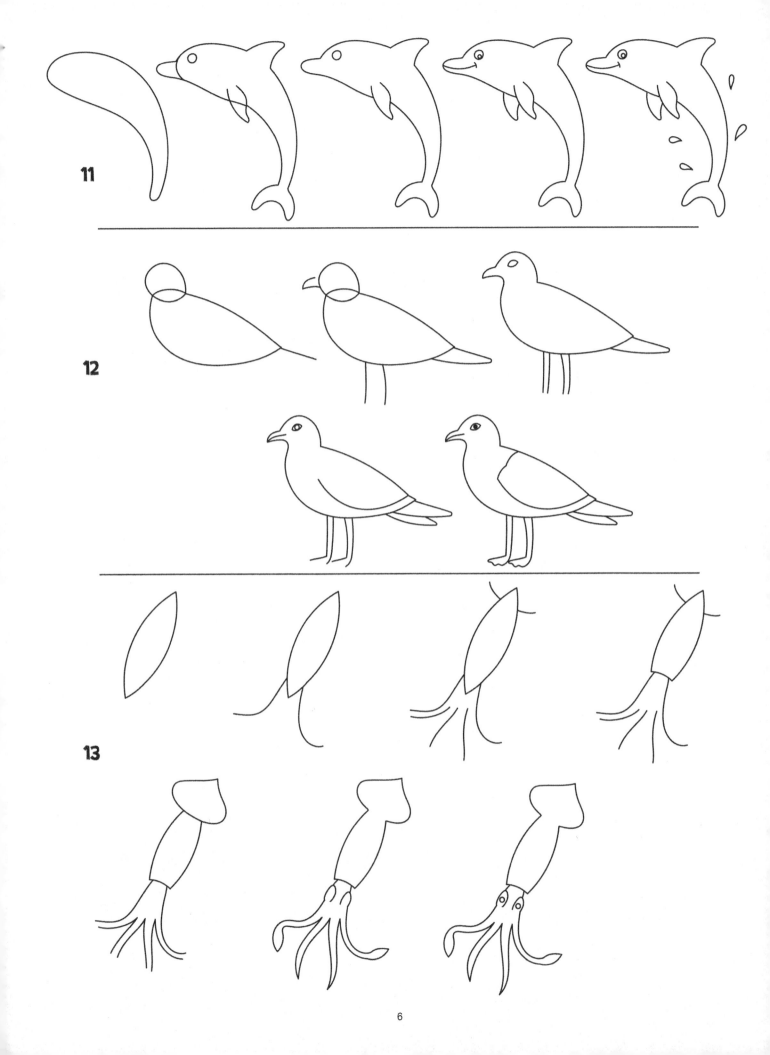

11

12

13

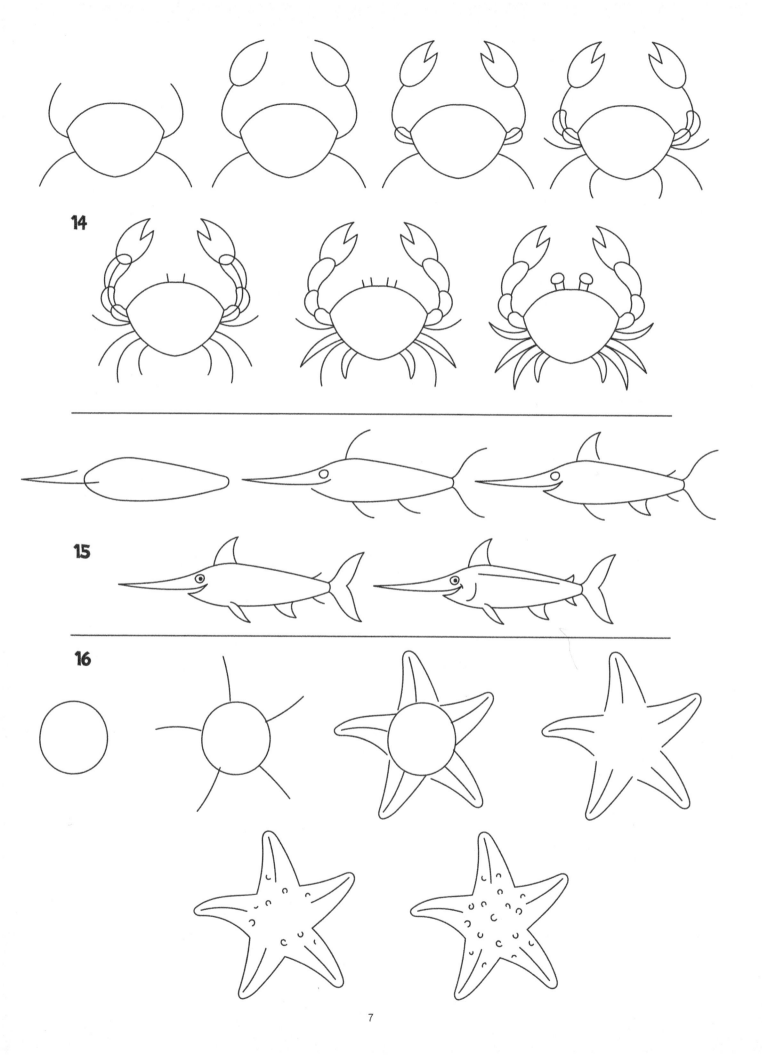

14

15

16

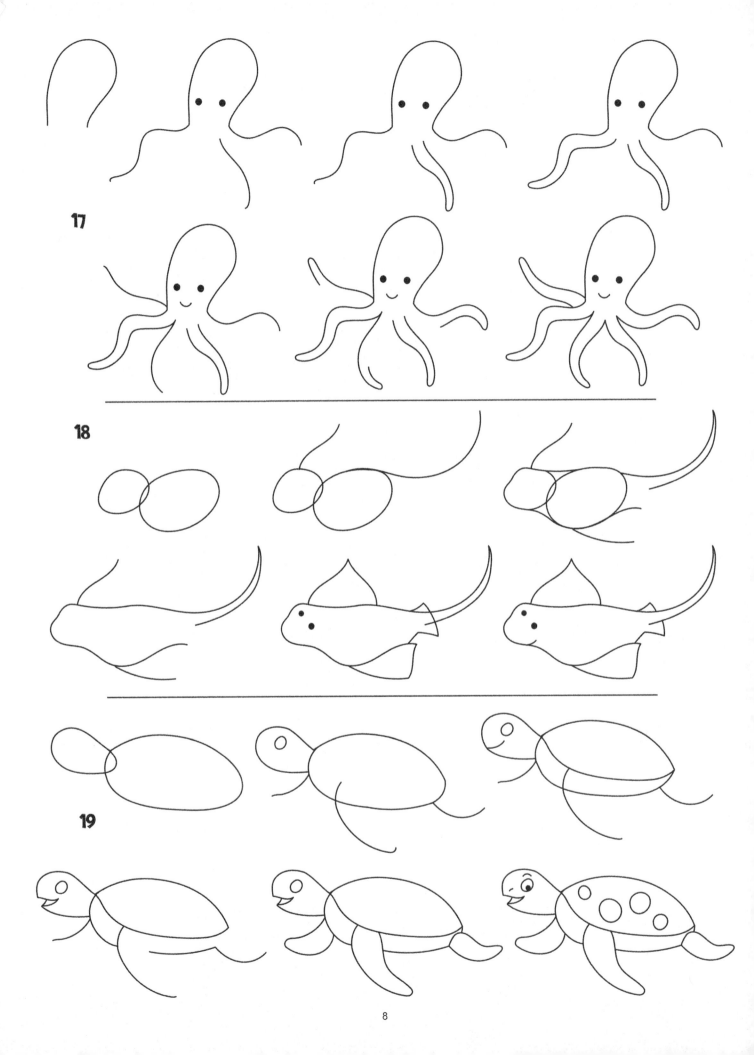

17

18

19

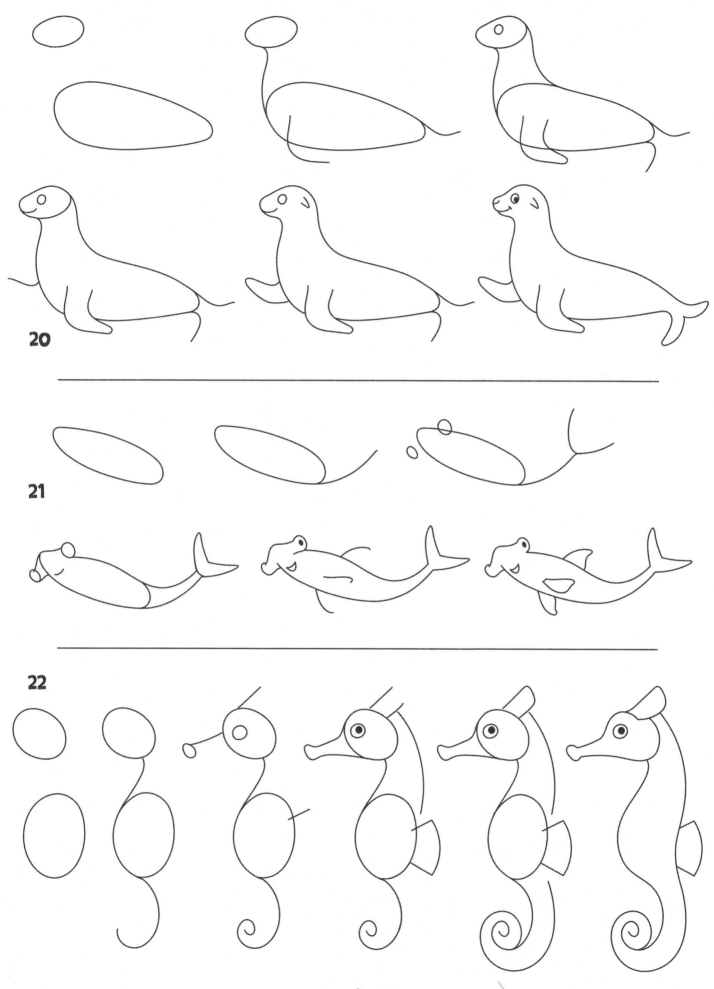

20

21

22

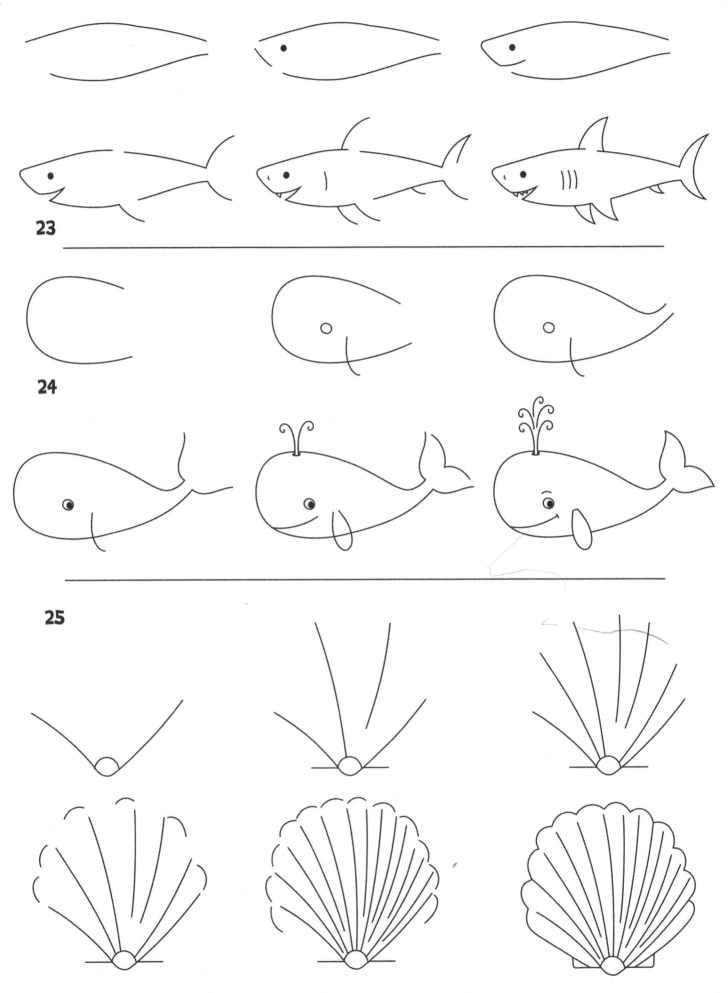

23

24

25

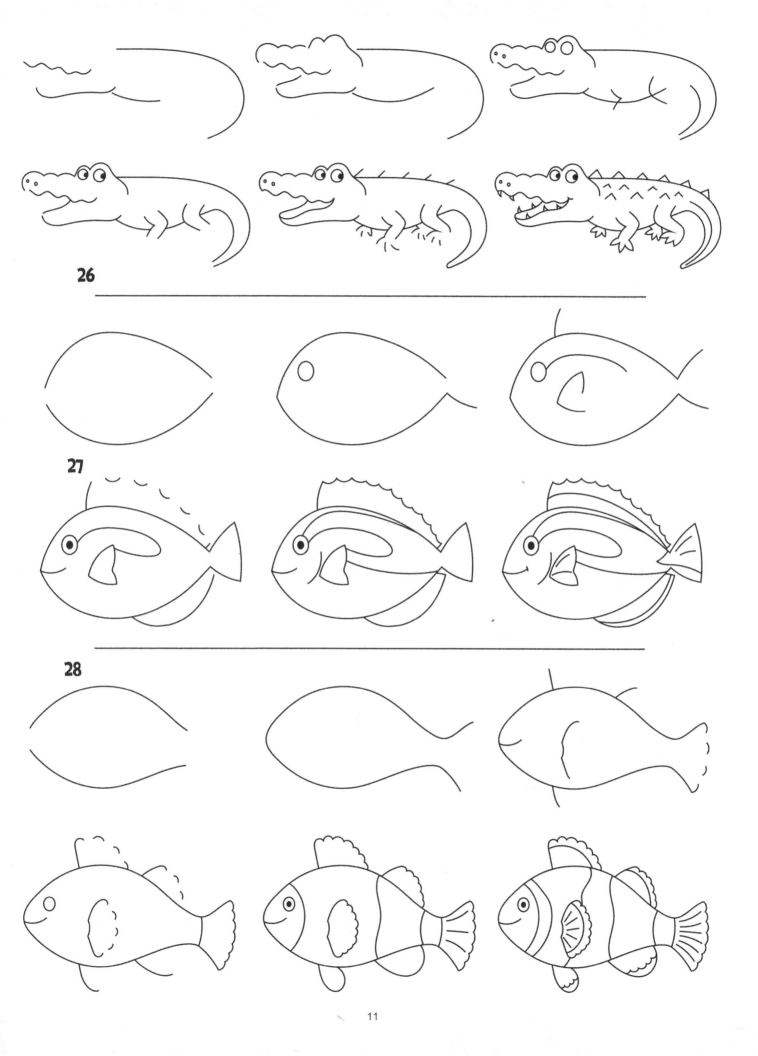

26

27

28

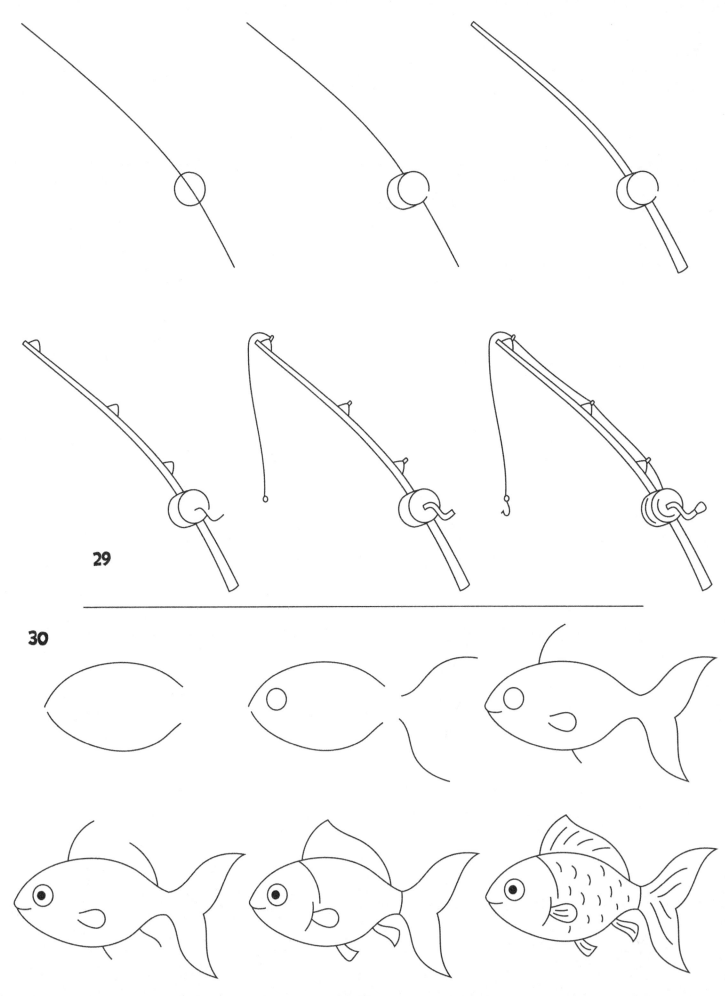

29

30

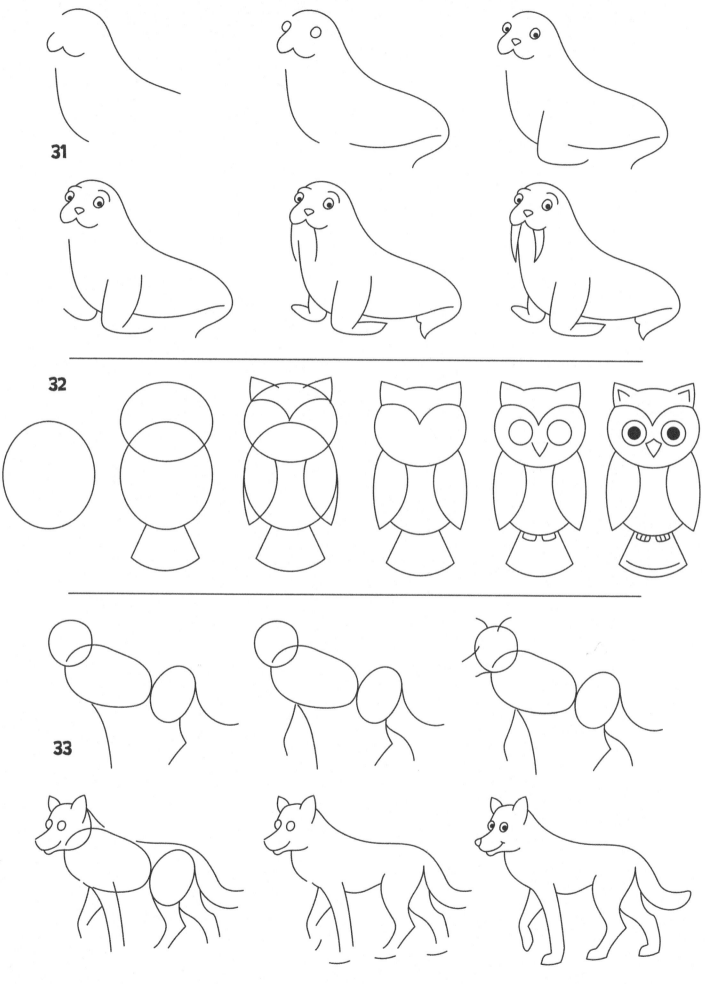

31

32

33

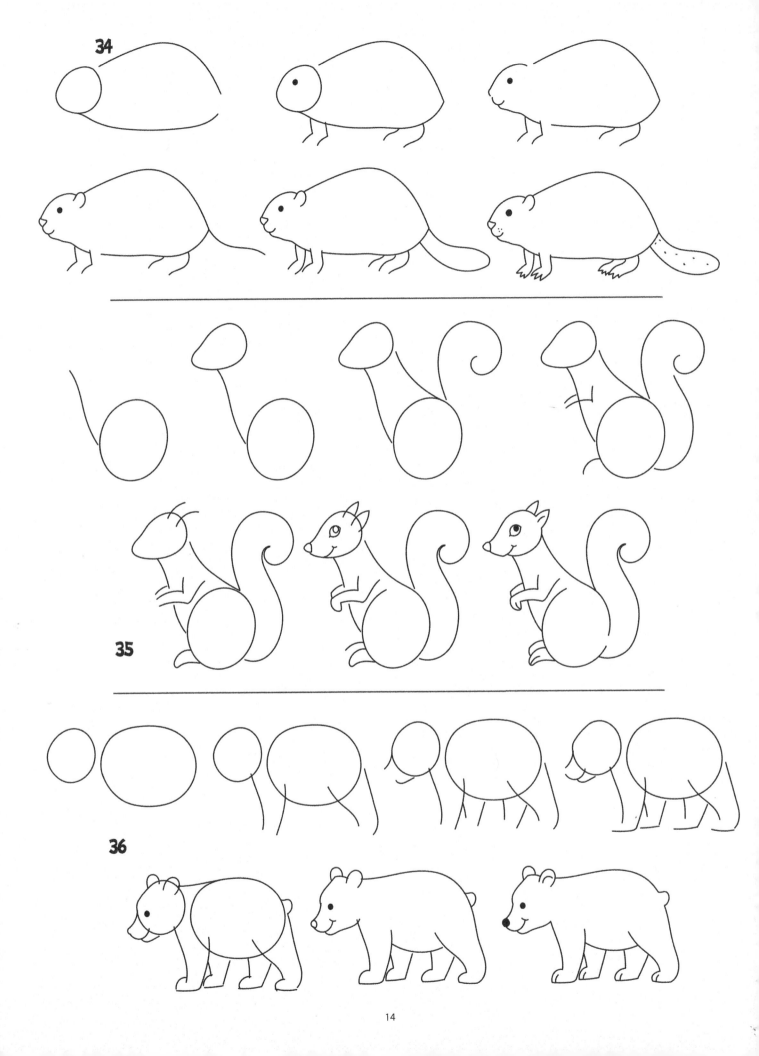

34

35

36

37

38

39

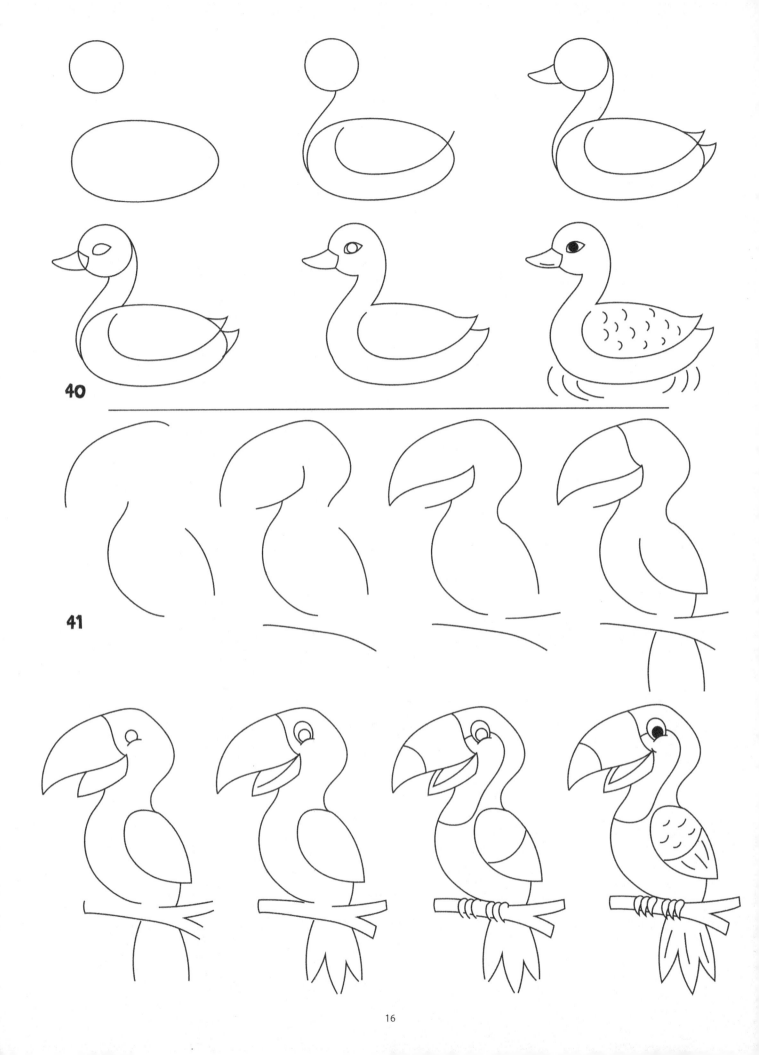

40

41

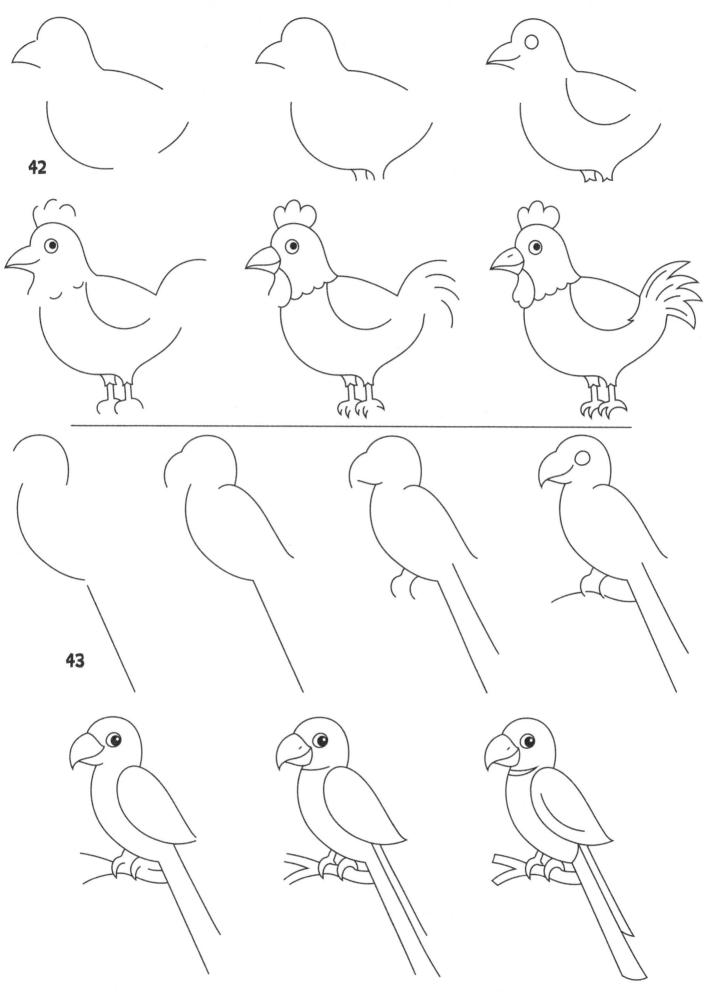

42

43

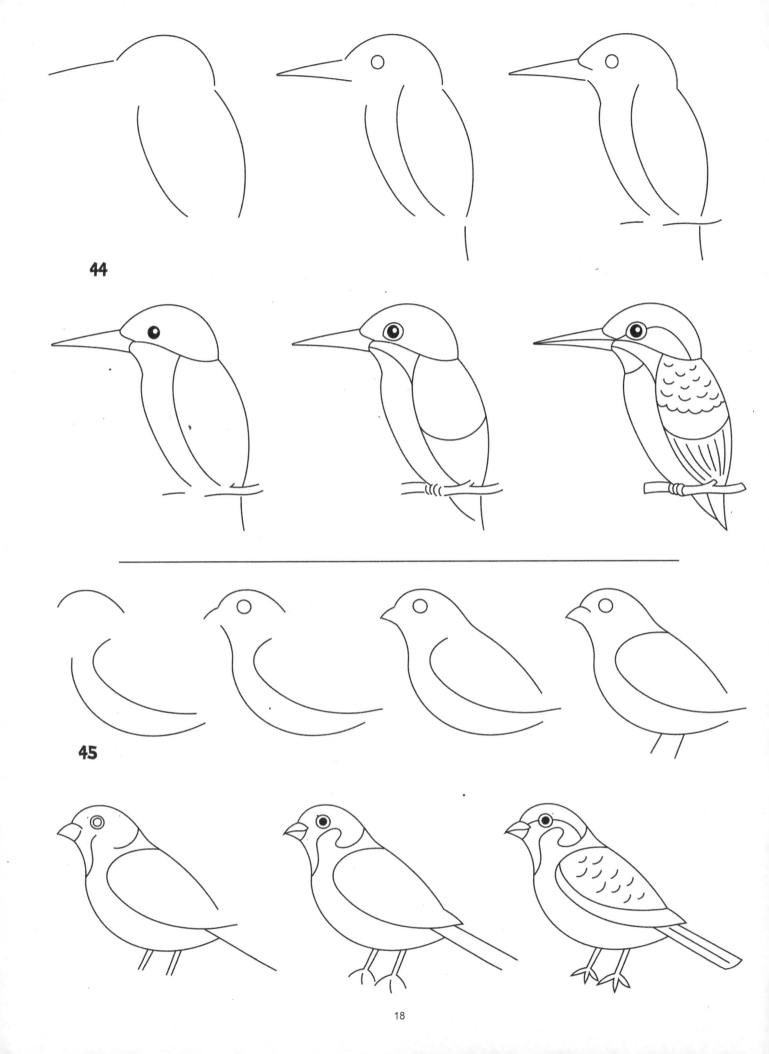

44

45

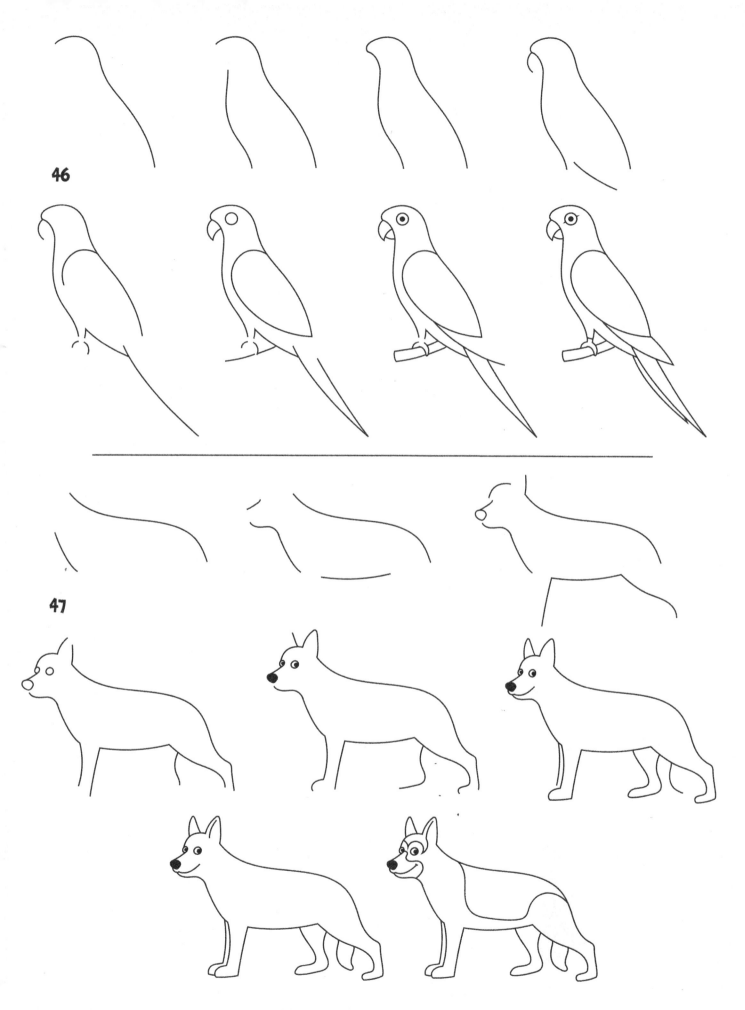

46

47

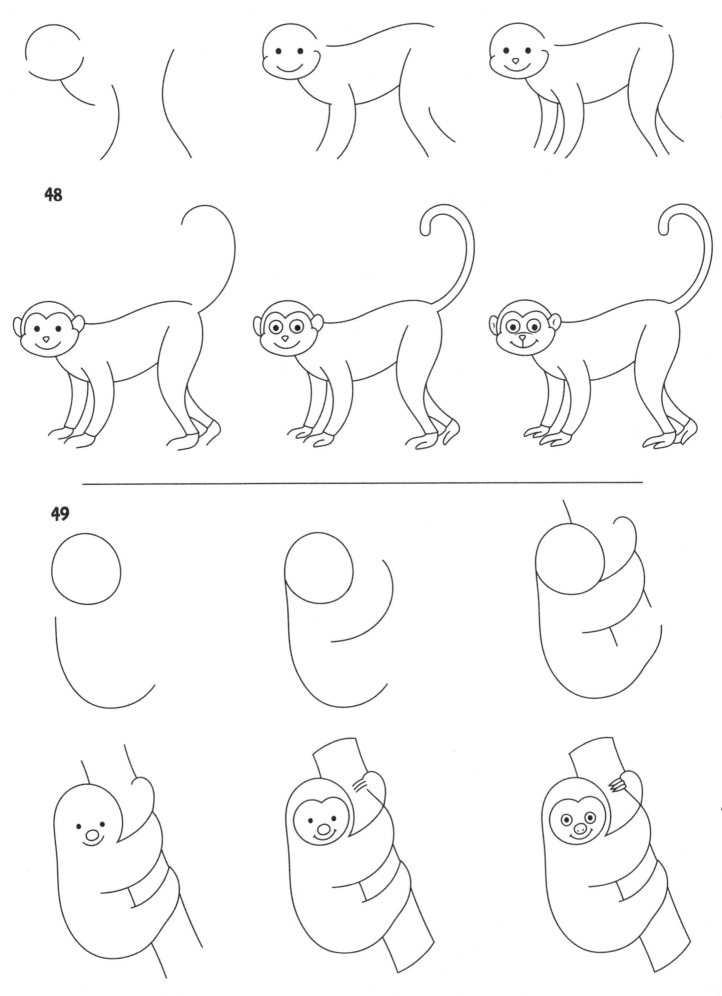

48

49

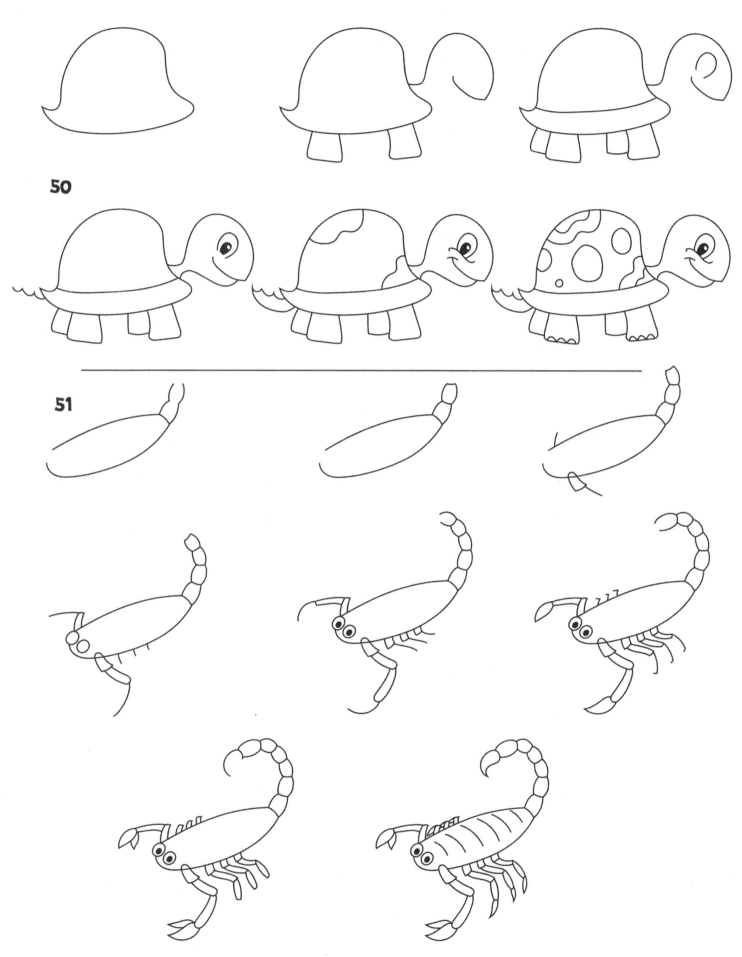

50

51

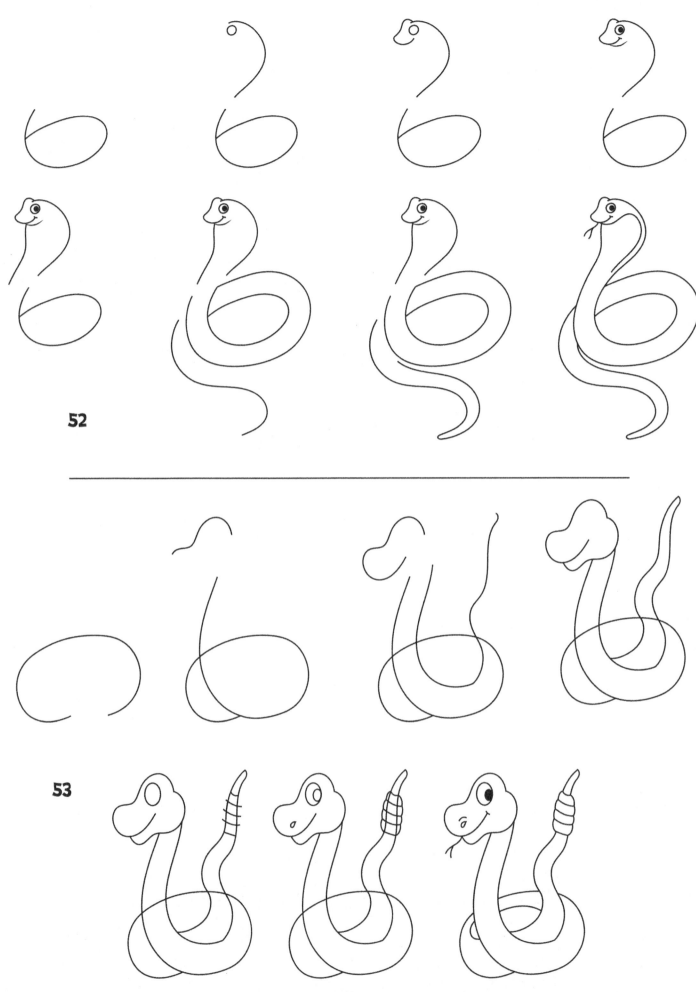

52

53

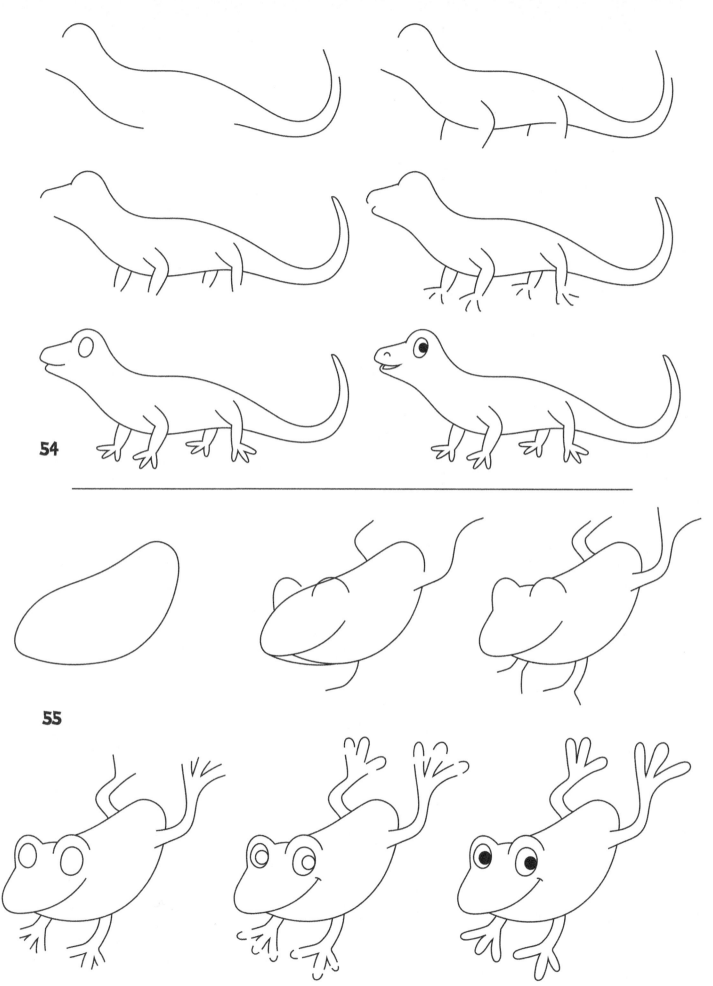

54

55

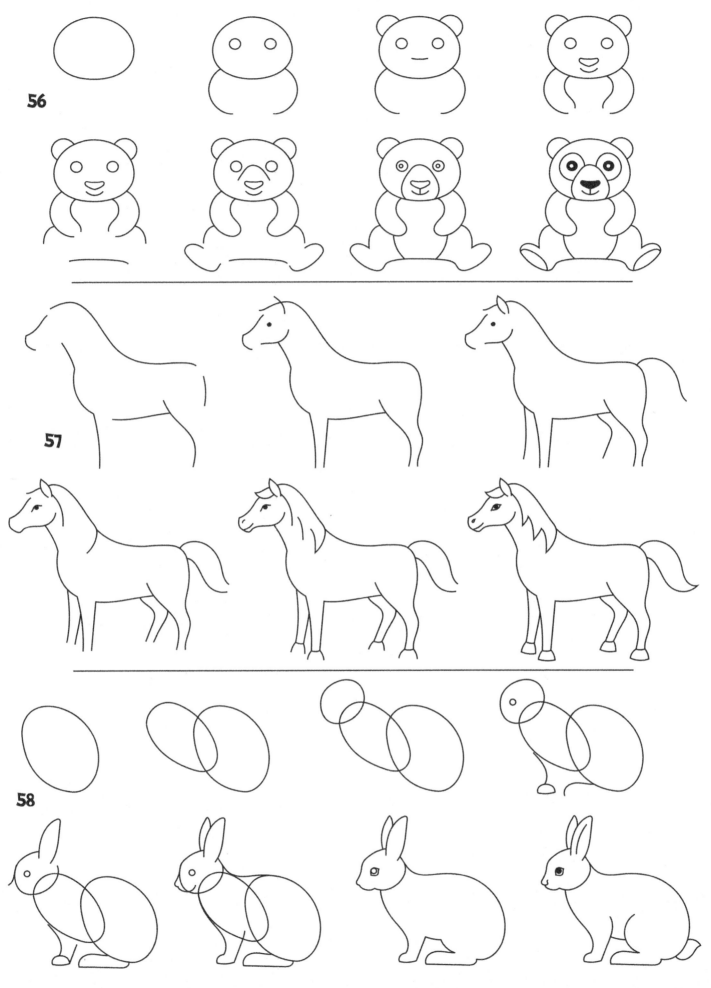

56

57

58

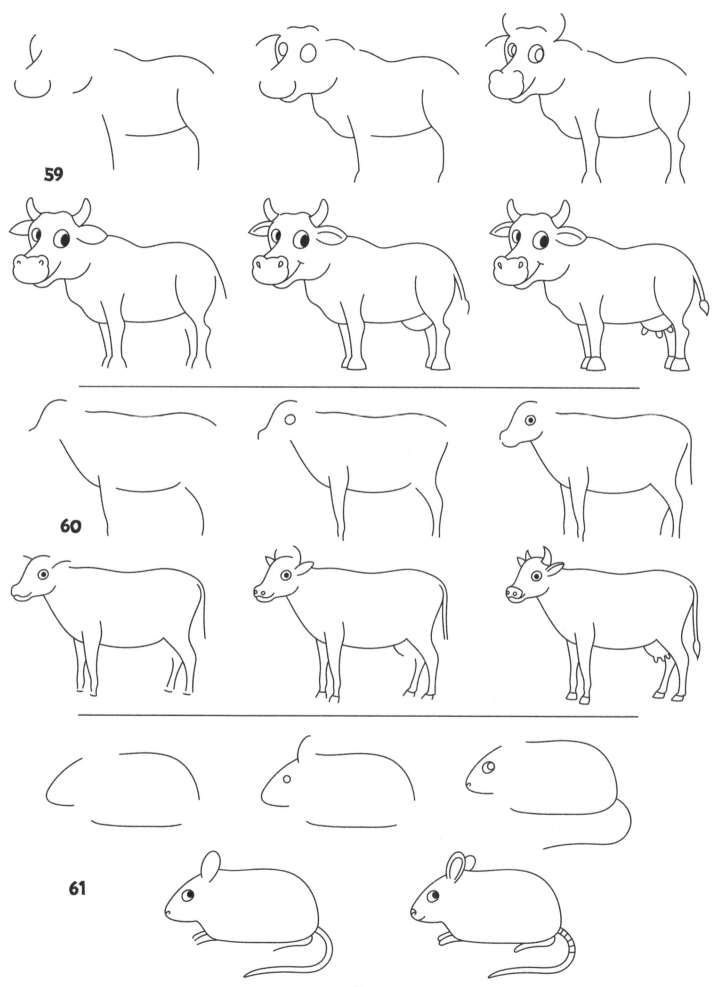

59

60

61

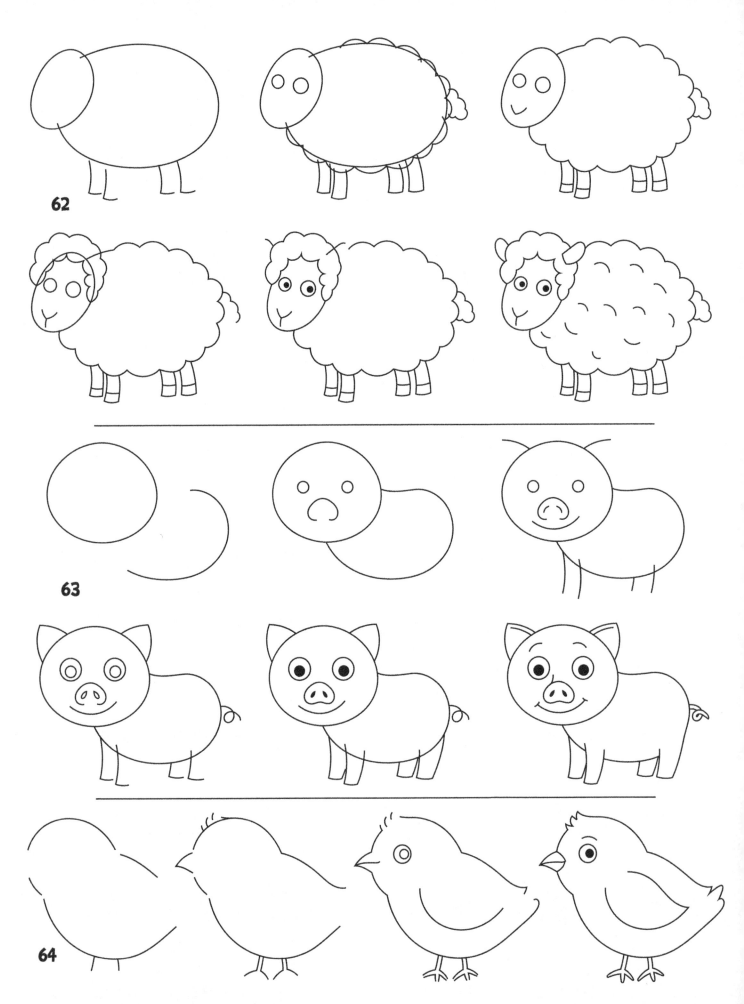

62

63

64

26

65

66

27

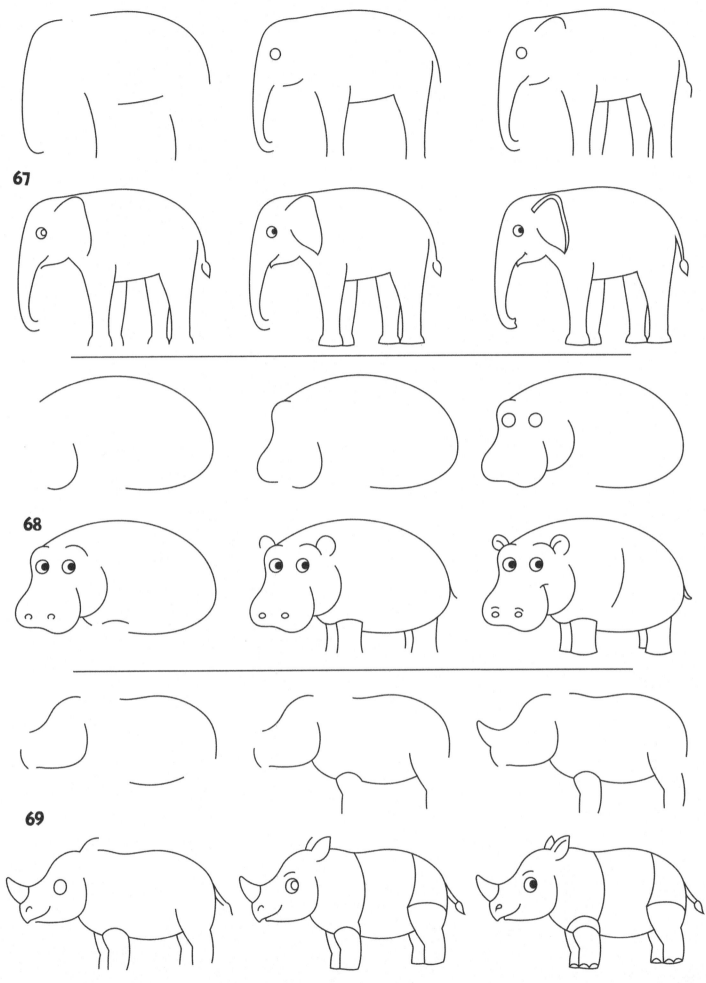

67

68

69

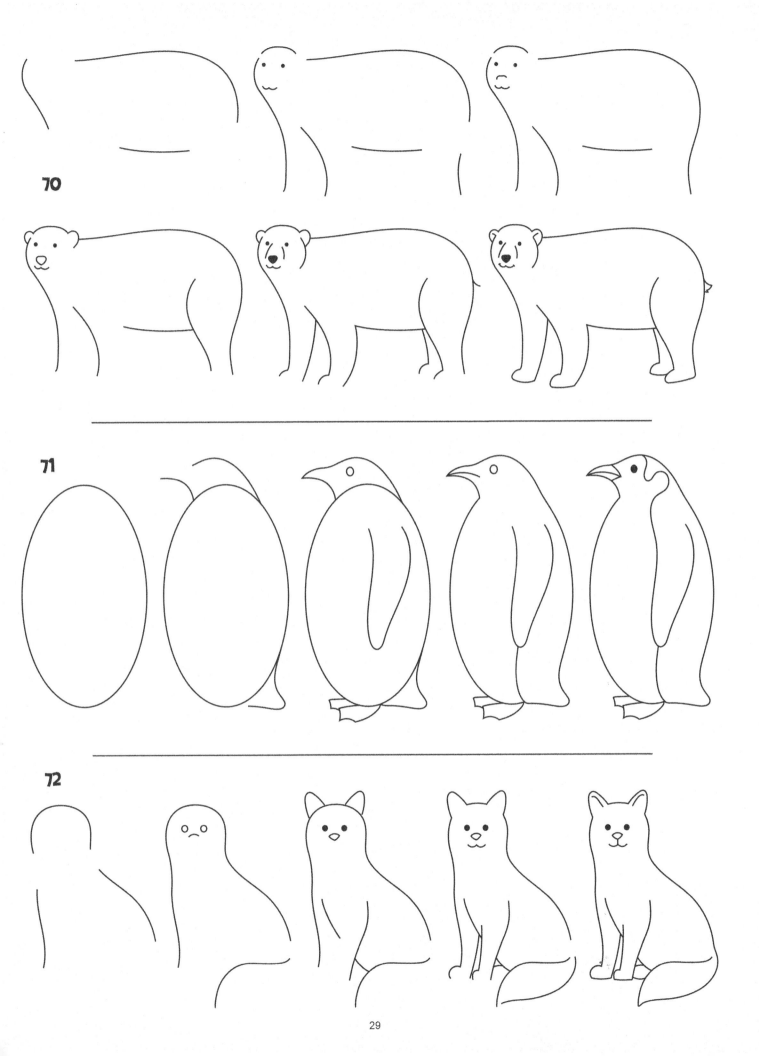

70

71

72

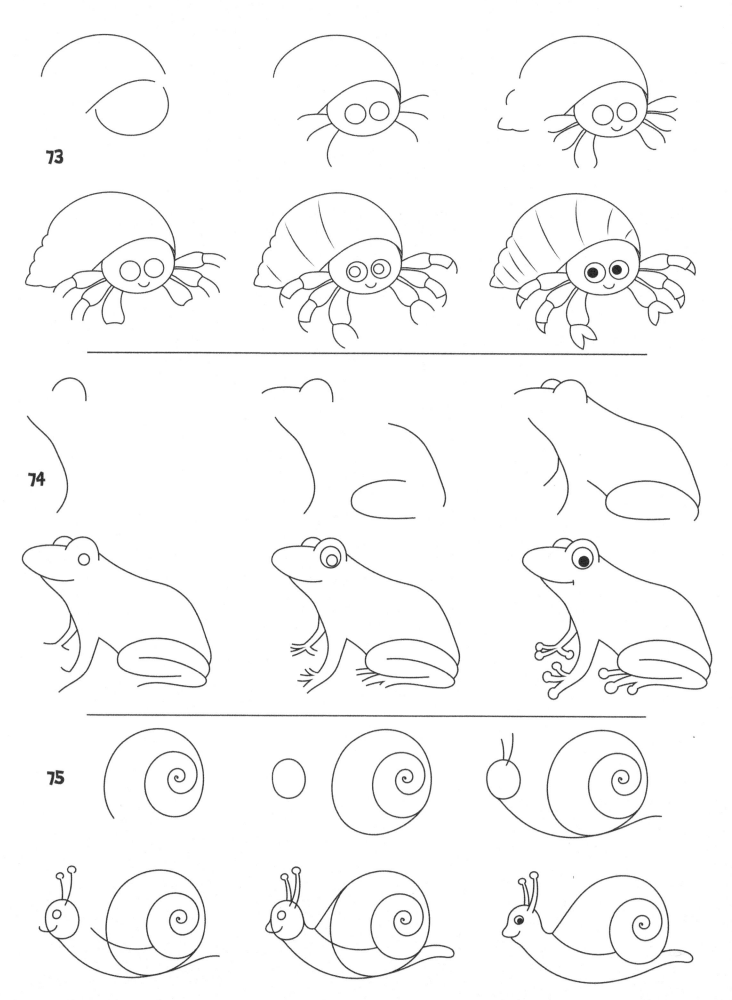

73

74

75

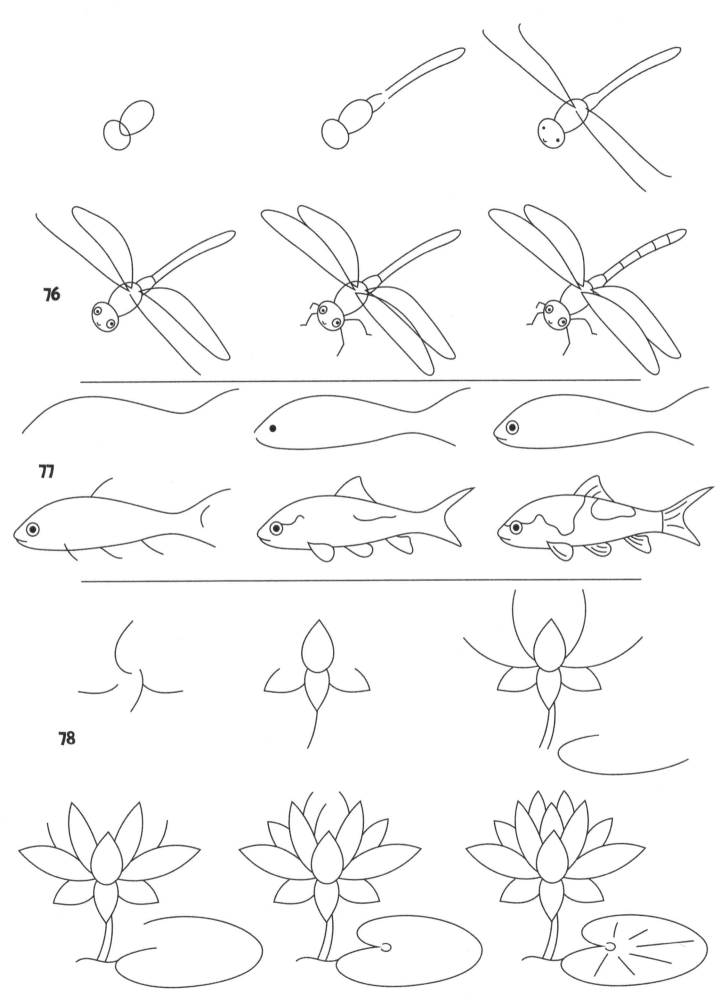

76

77

78

79

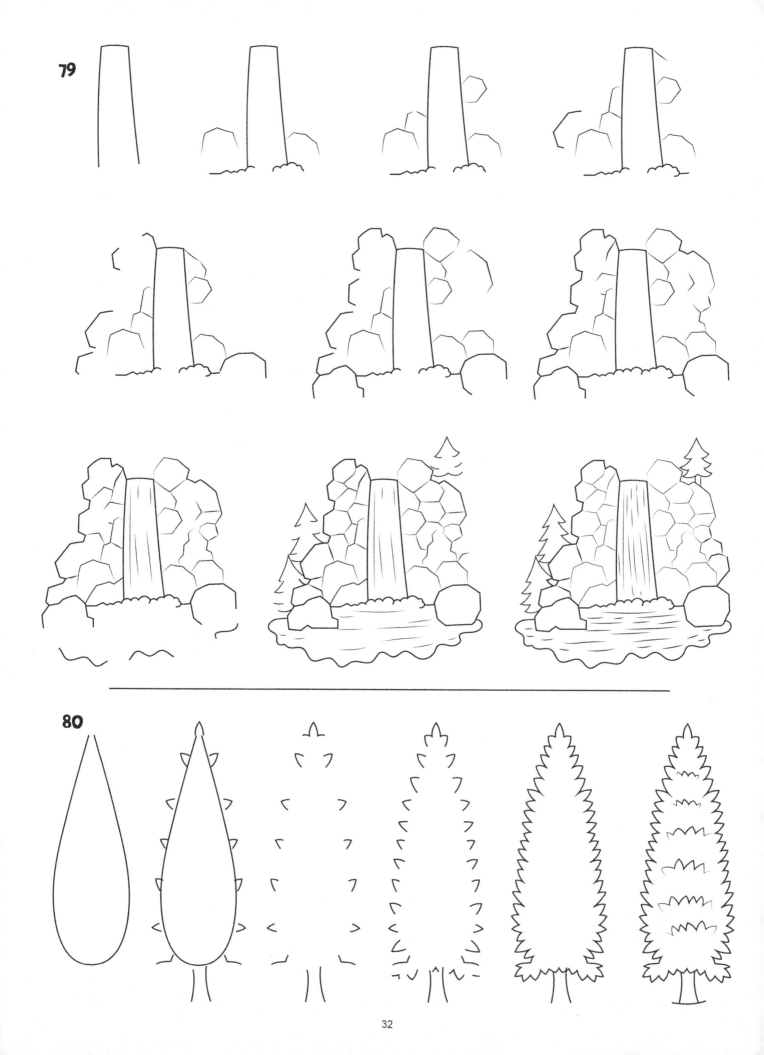

80

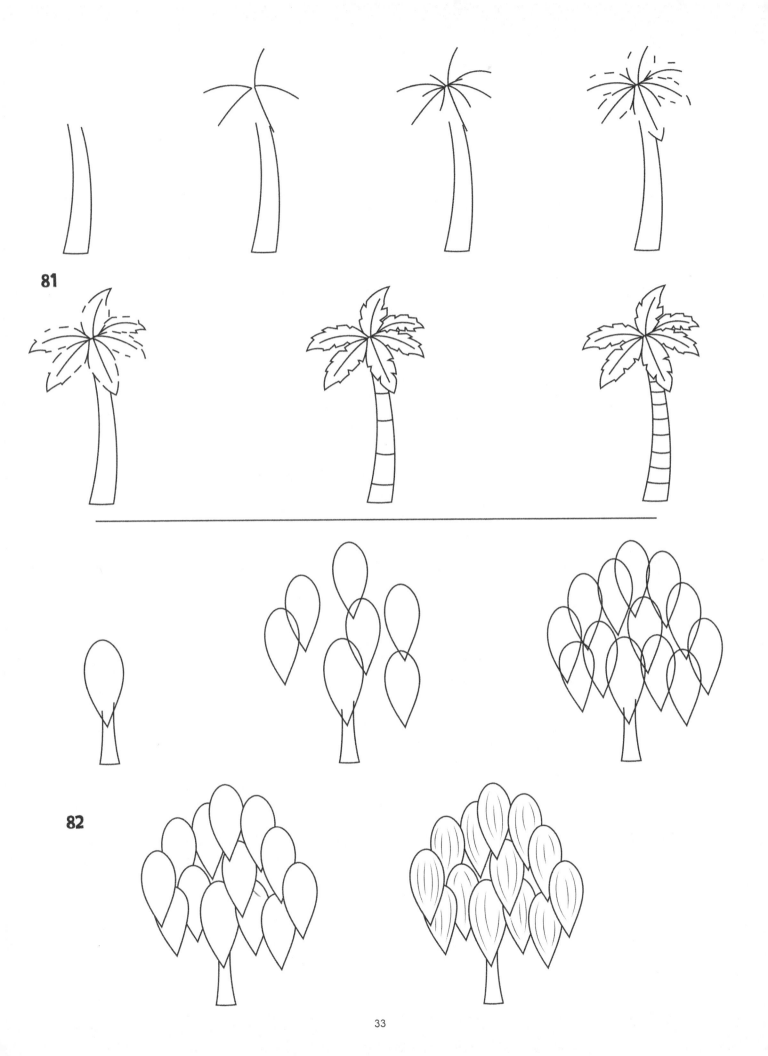

81

82

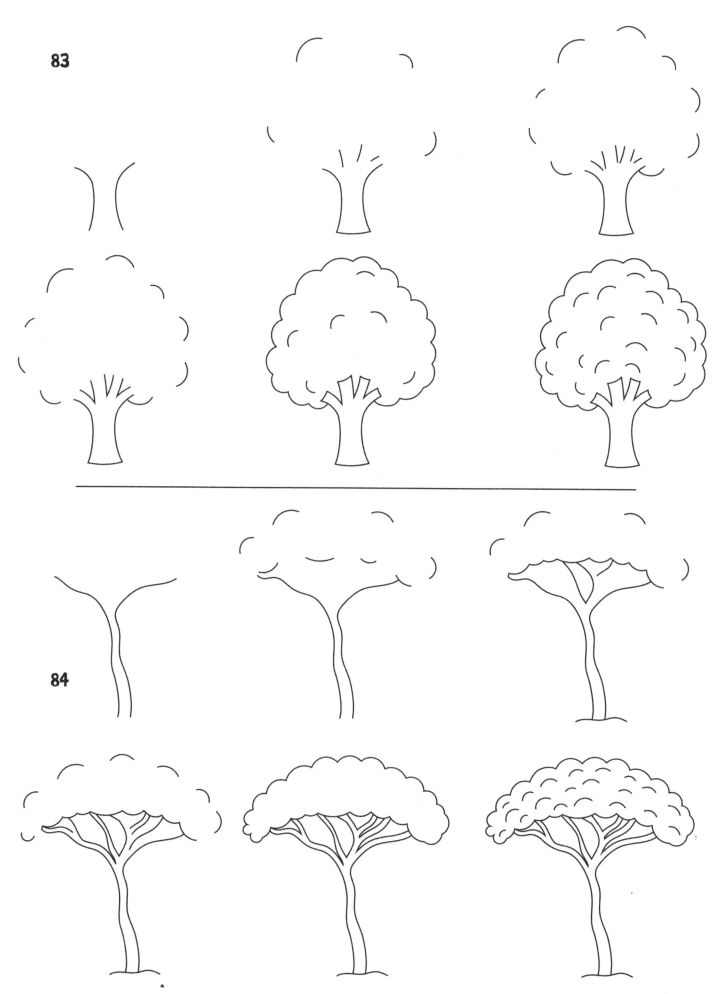

83

84

85

86

87

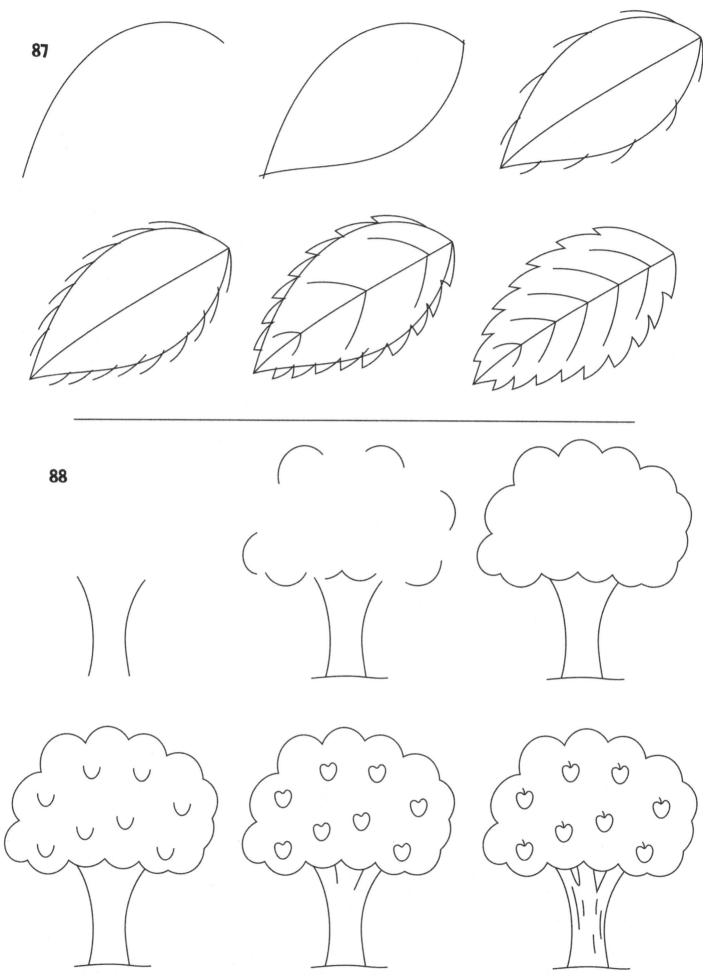

88

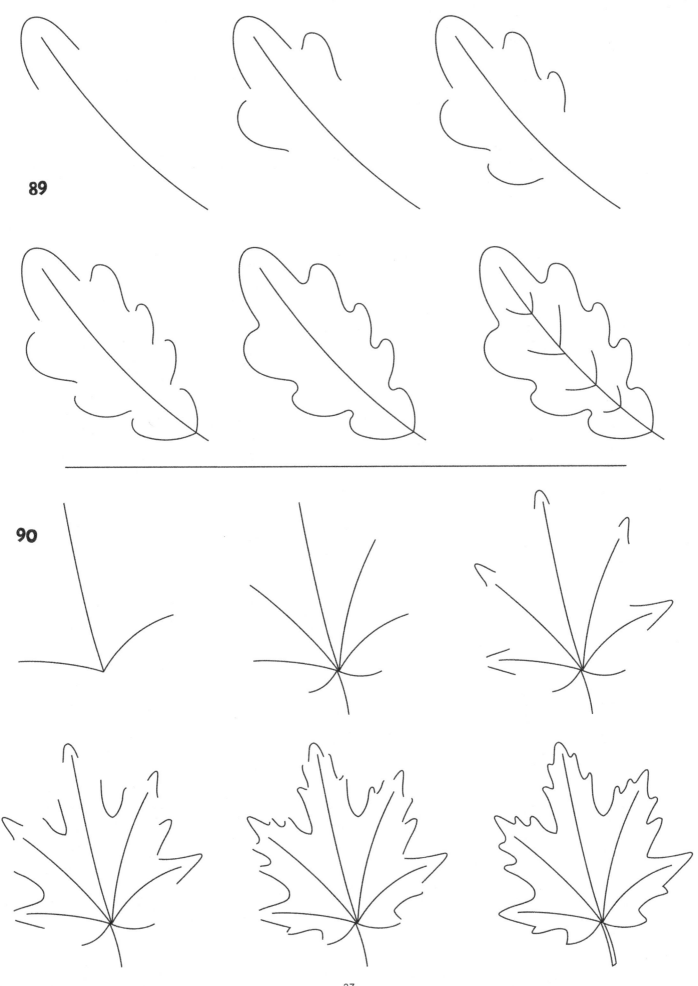

89

90

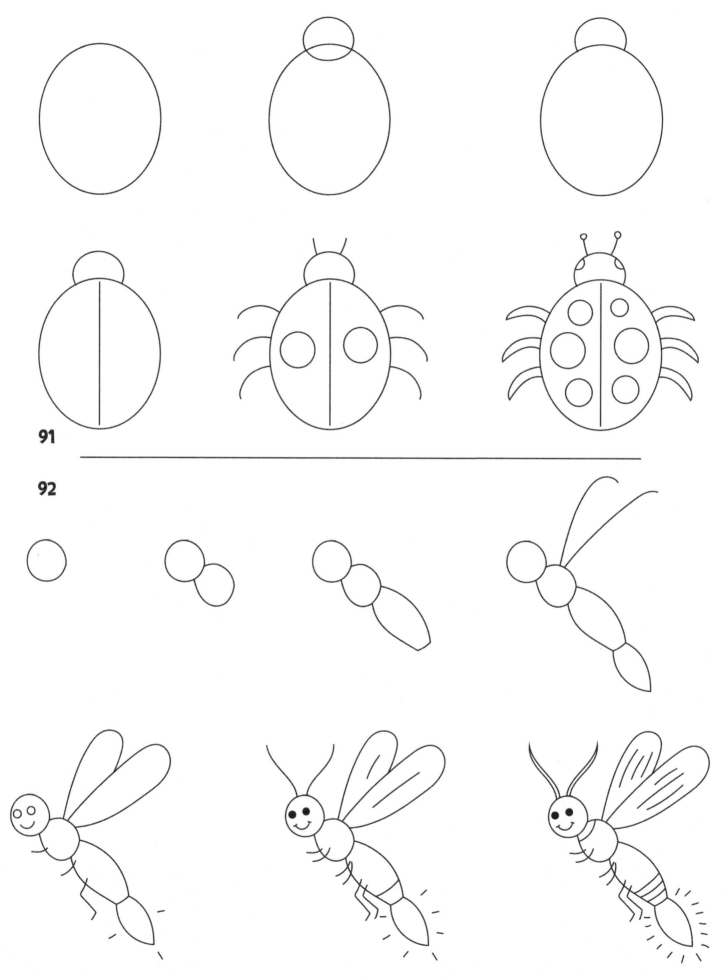

91

92

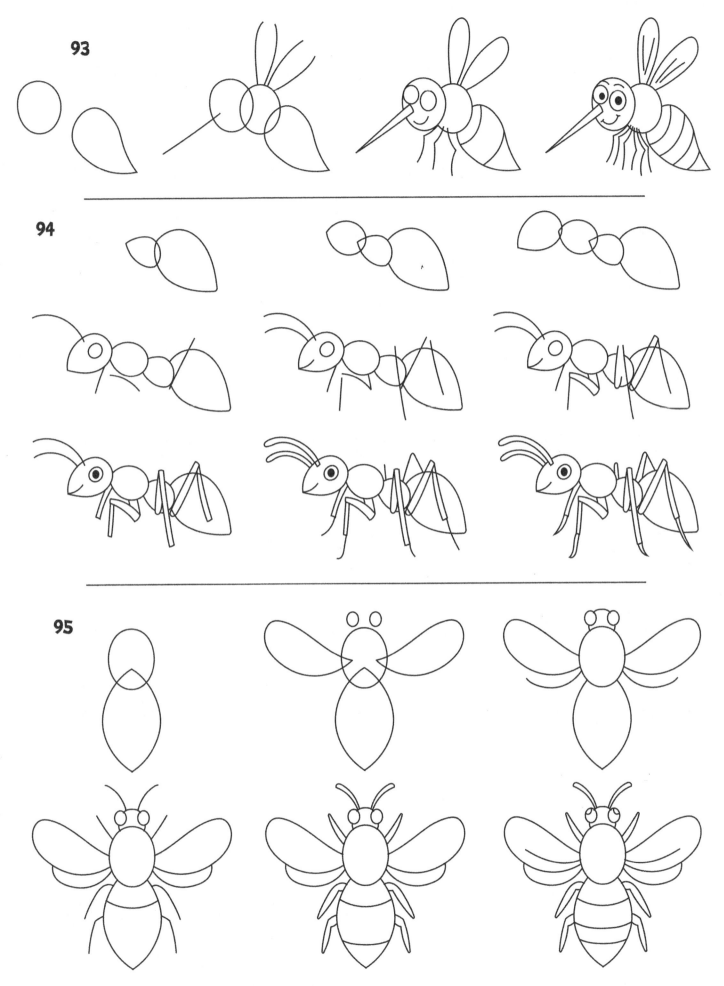

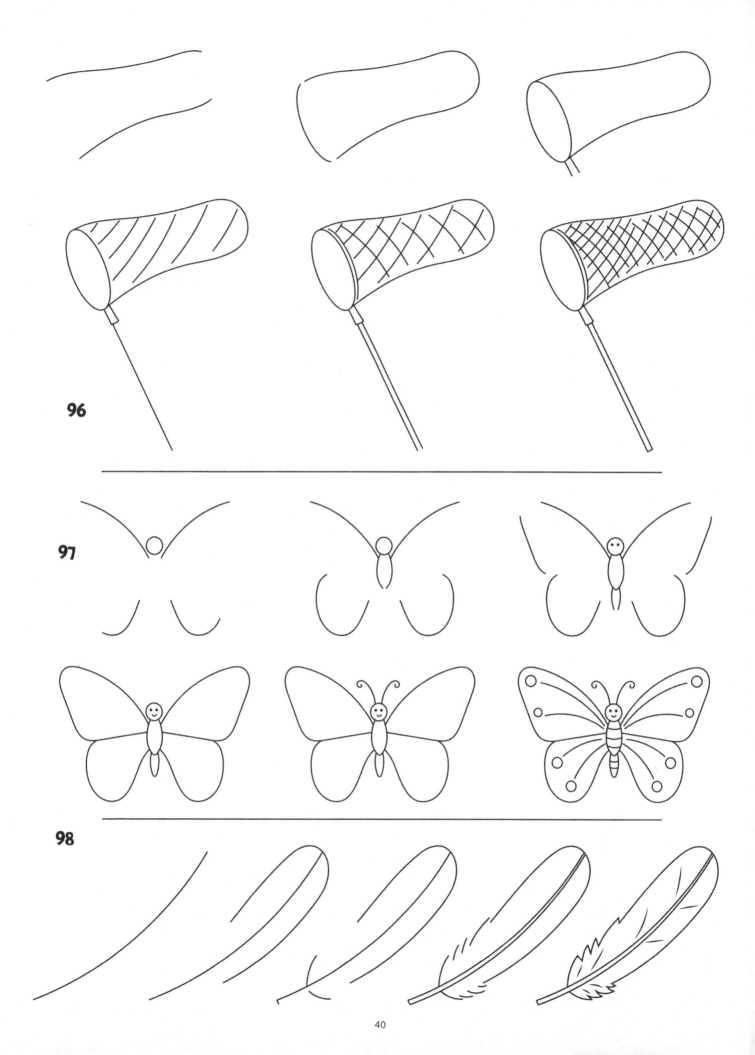

96

97

98

40

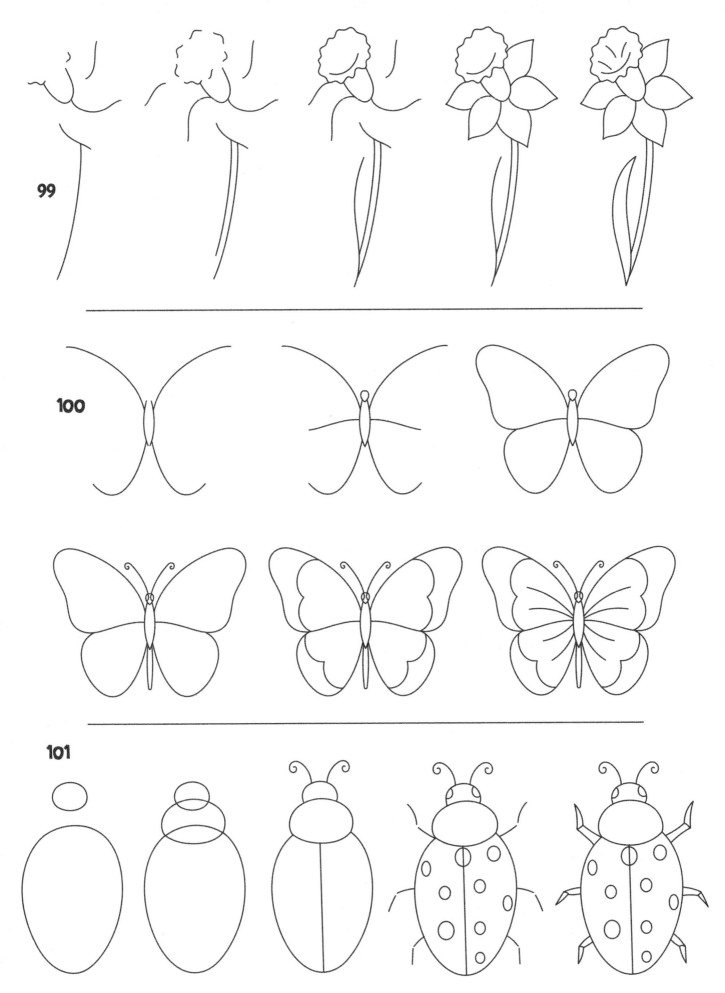

99

100

101

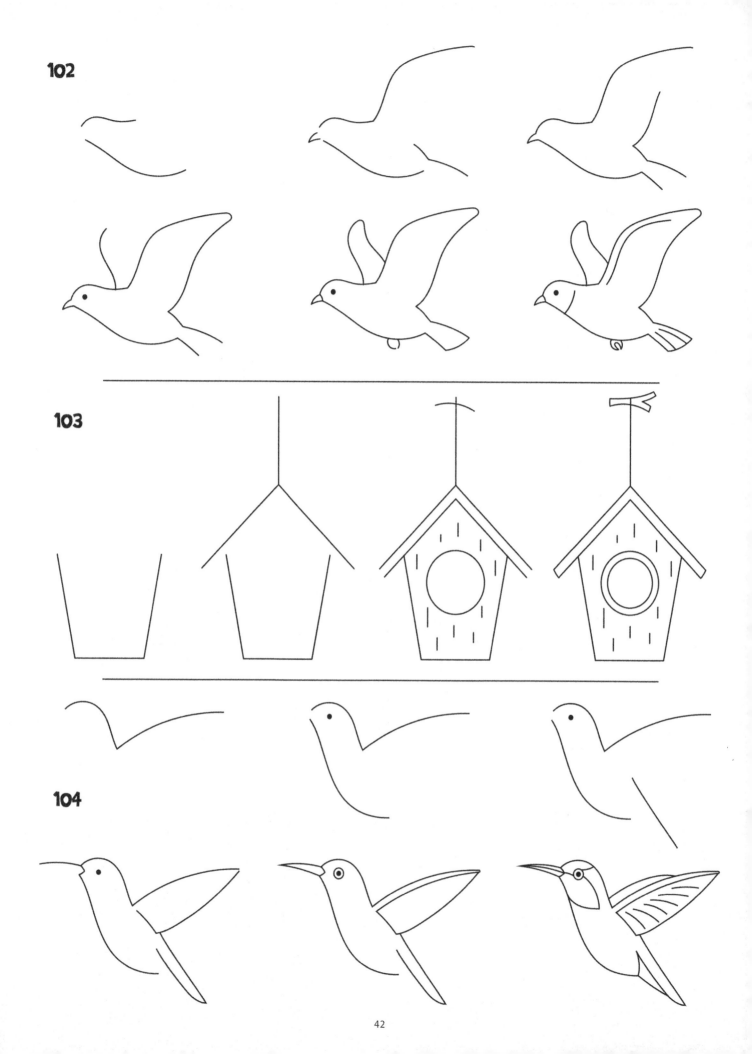

102

103

104

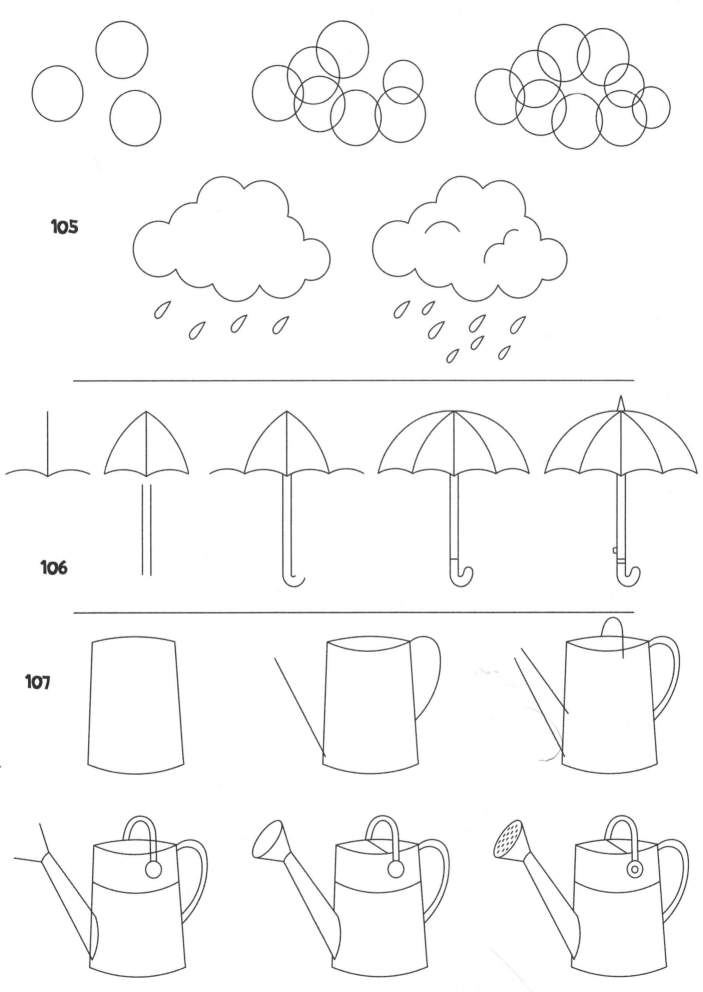

105

106

107

43

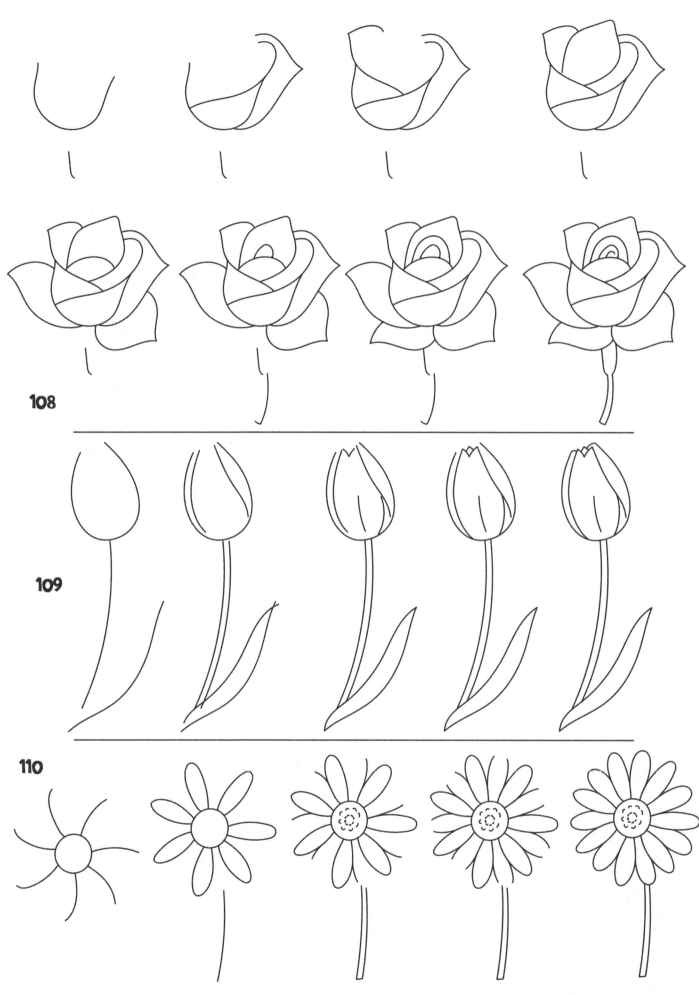

108

109

110

44

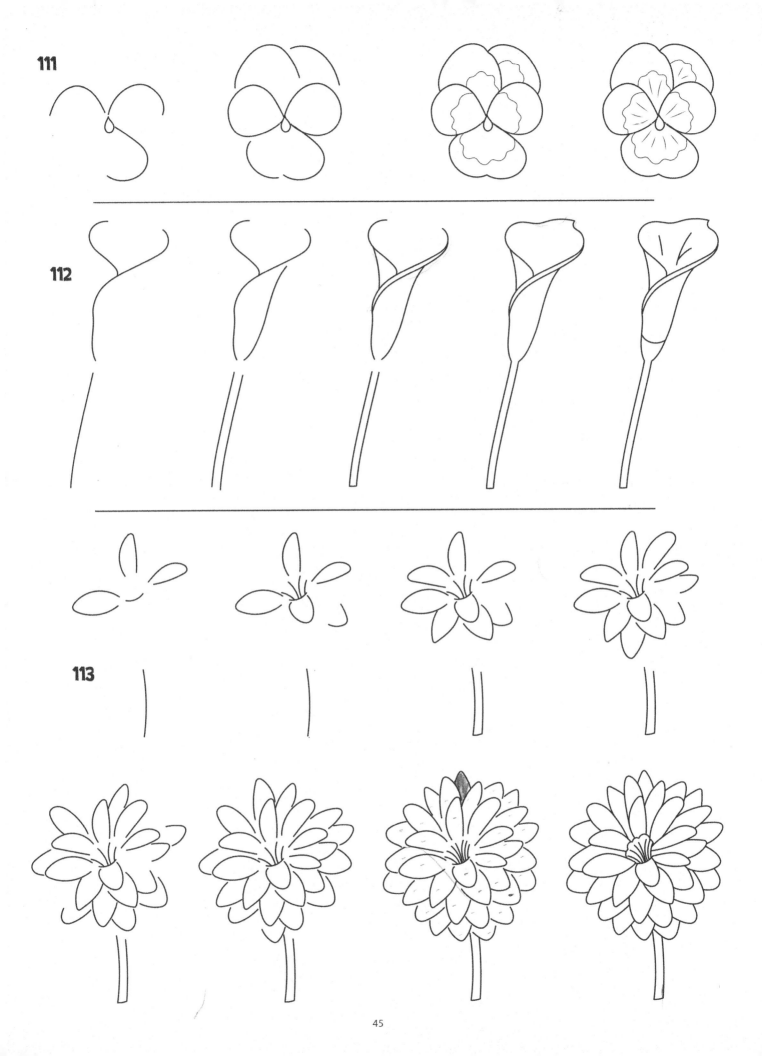

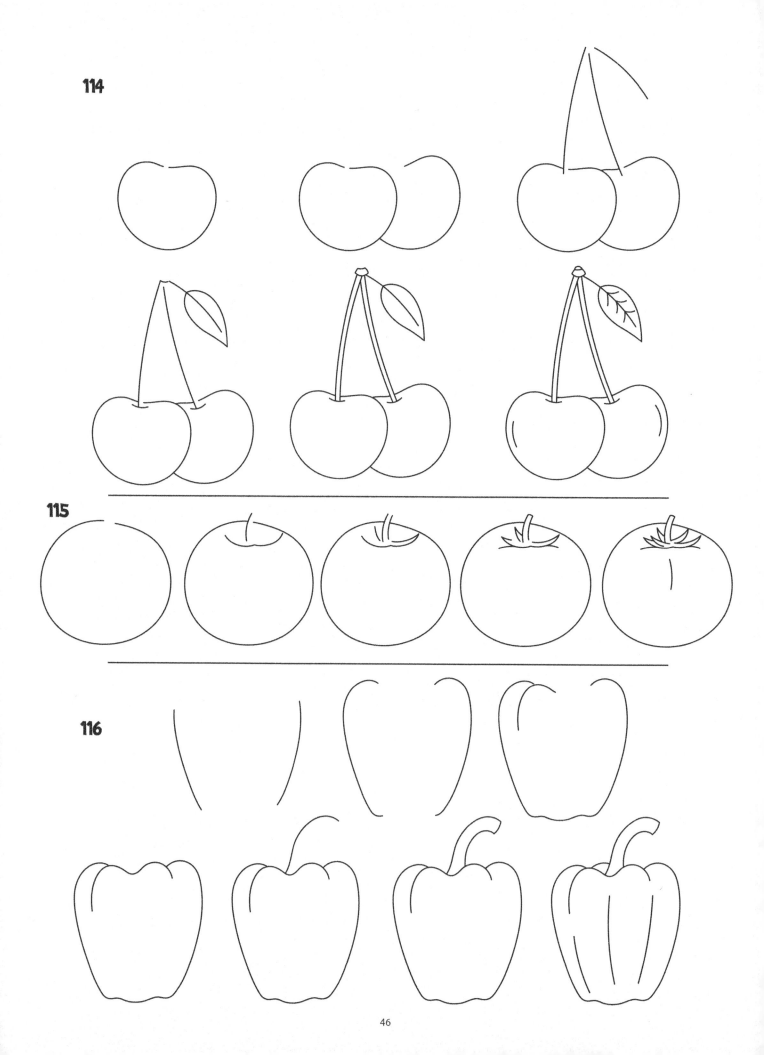

114

115

116

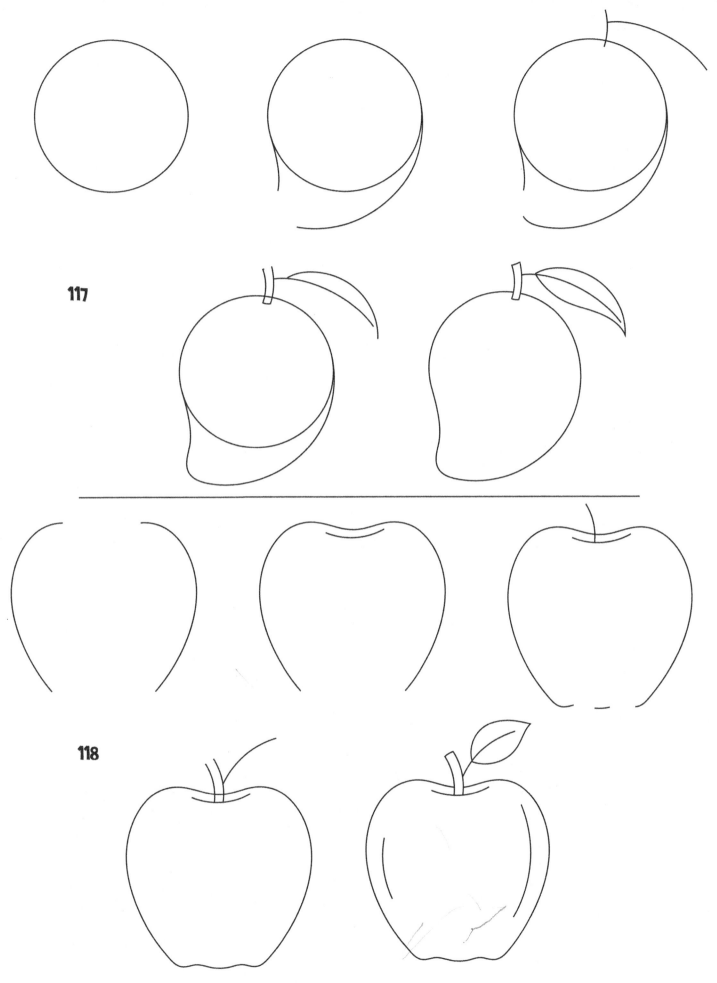

117

118

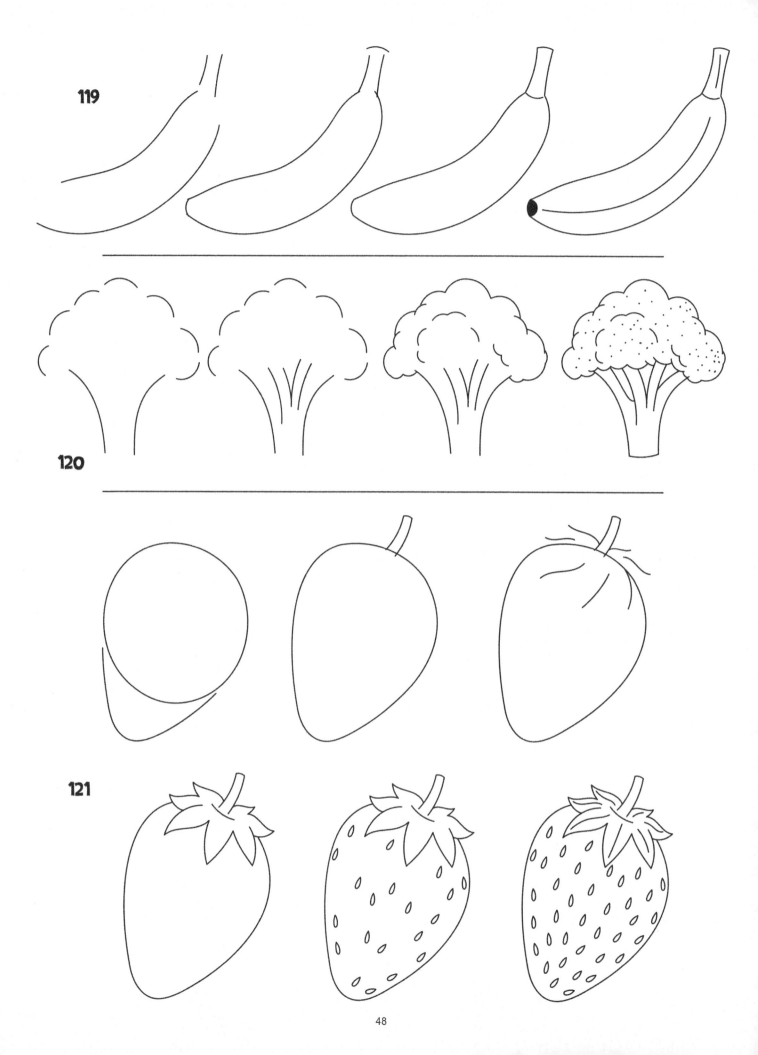

119

120

121

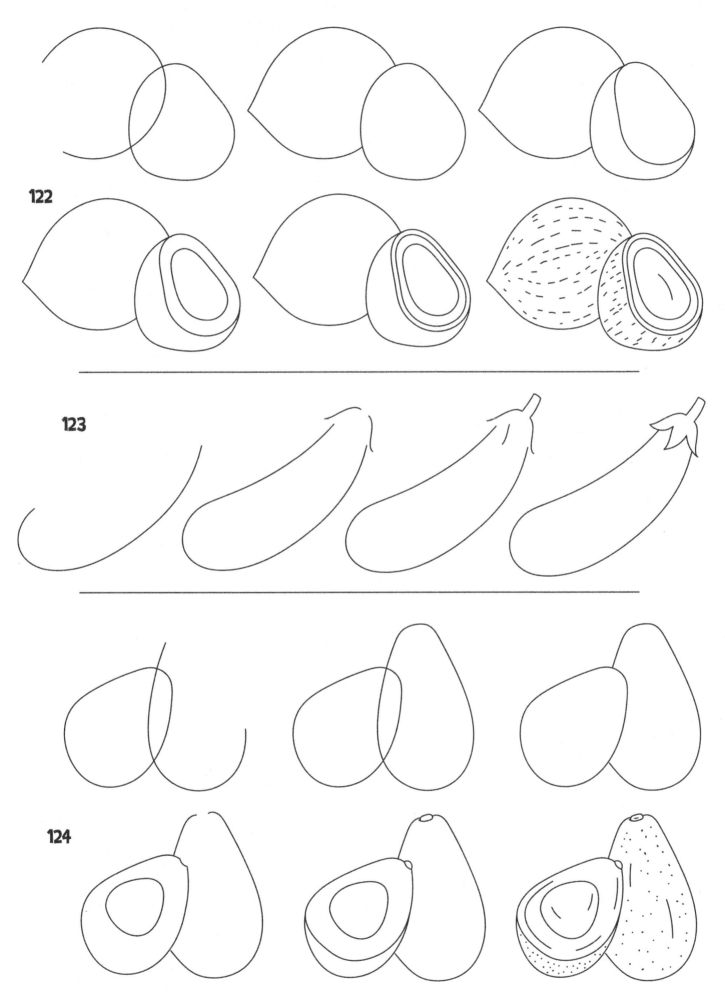

122

123

124

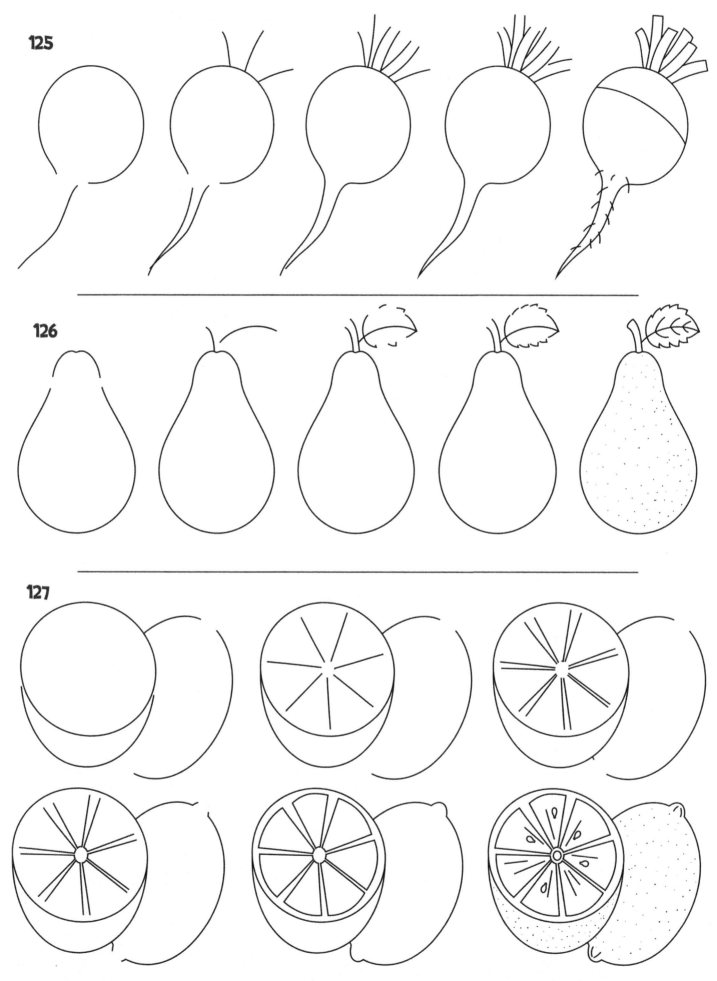

125

126

127

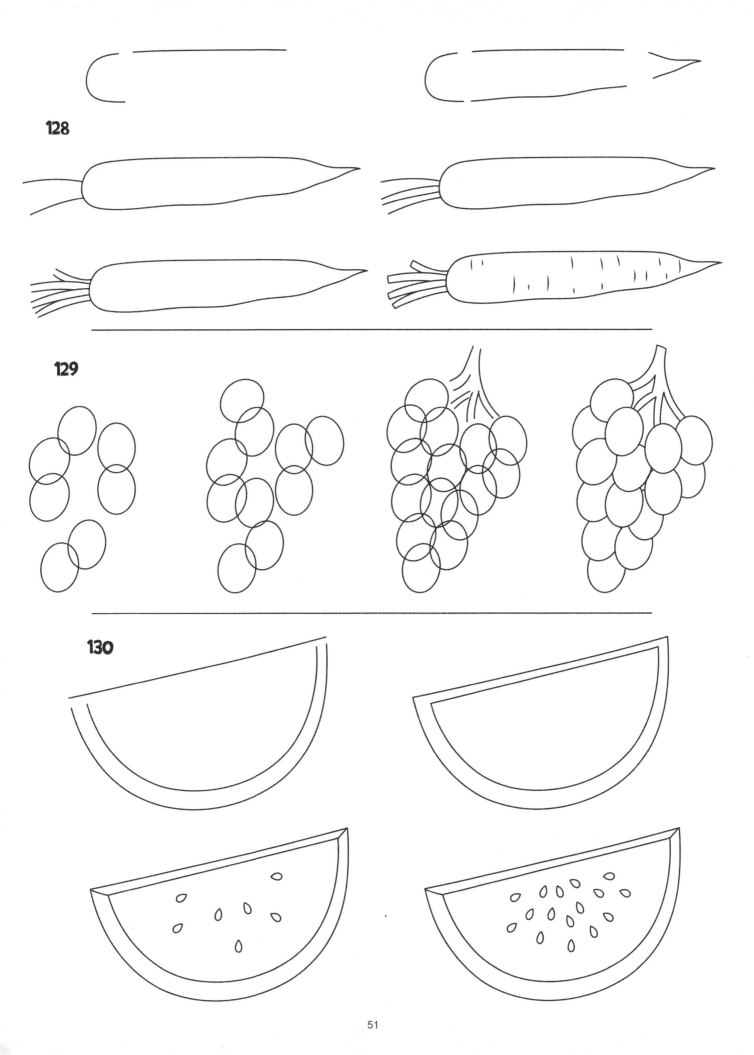

128

129

130

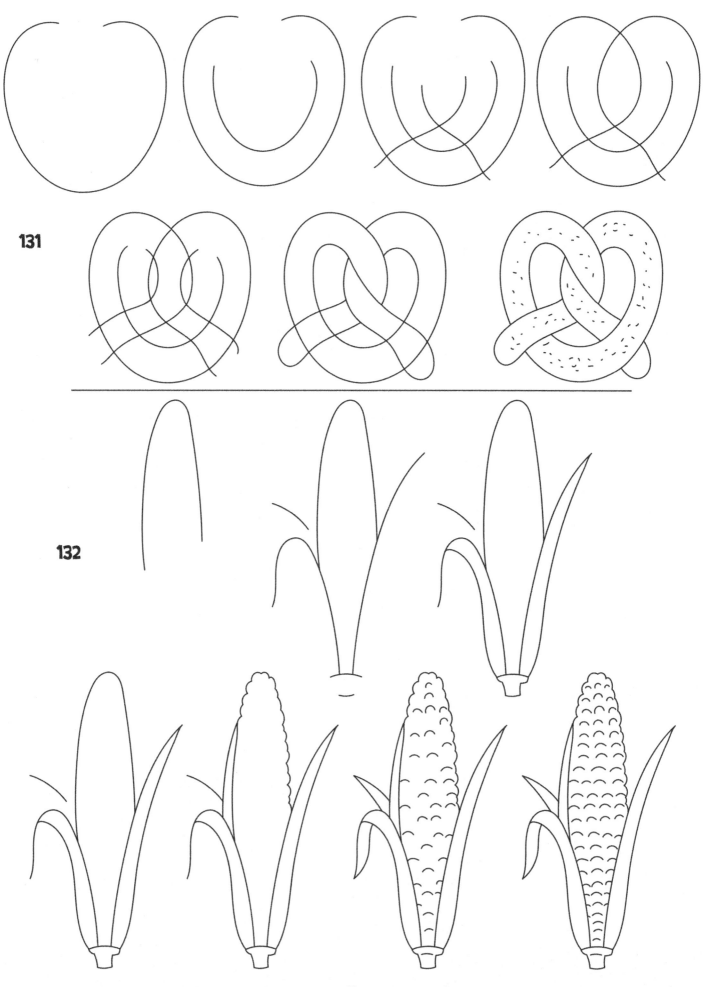

131

132

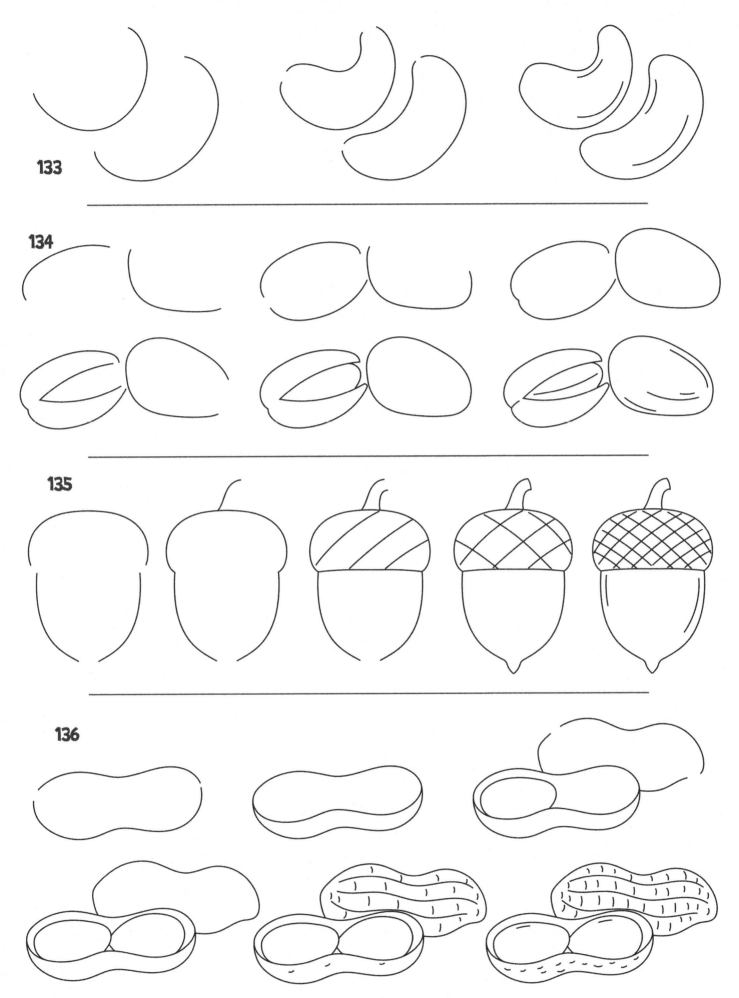

133

134

135

136

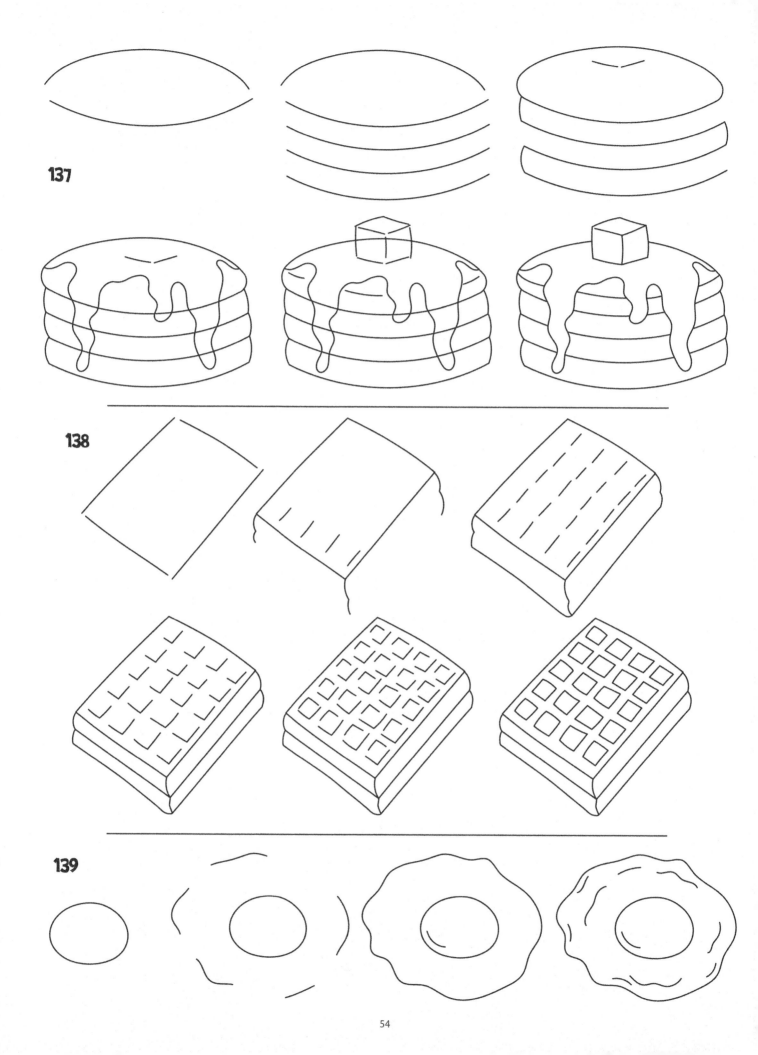

137

138

139

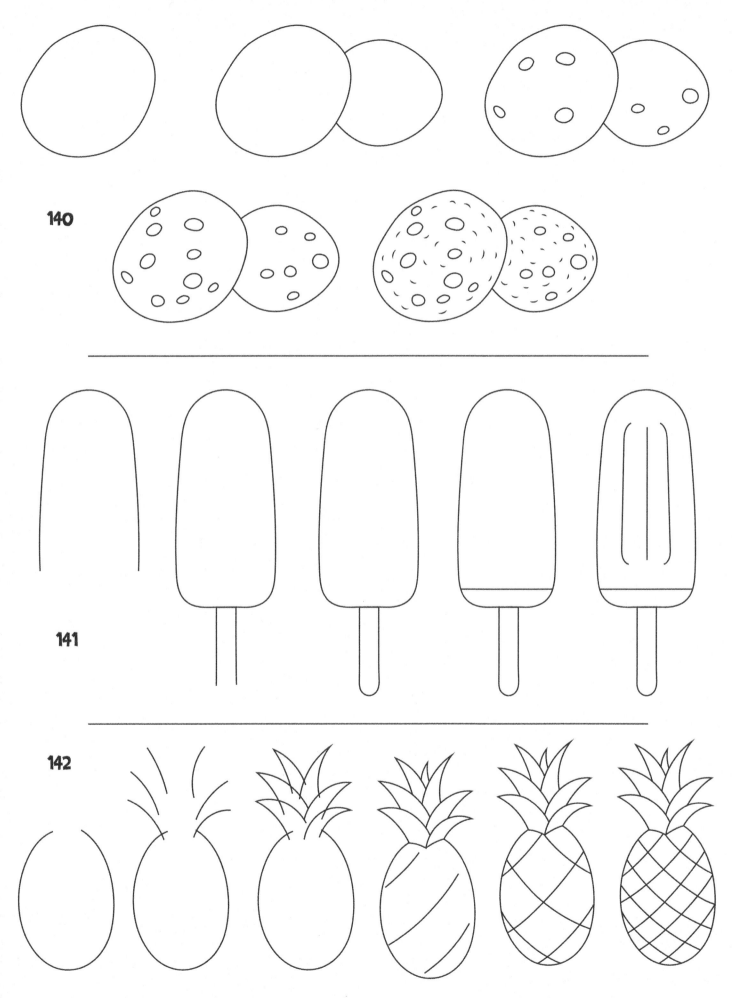

140

141

142

143

144

145

146

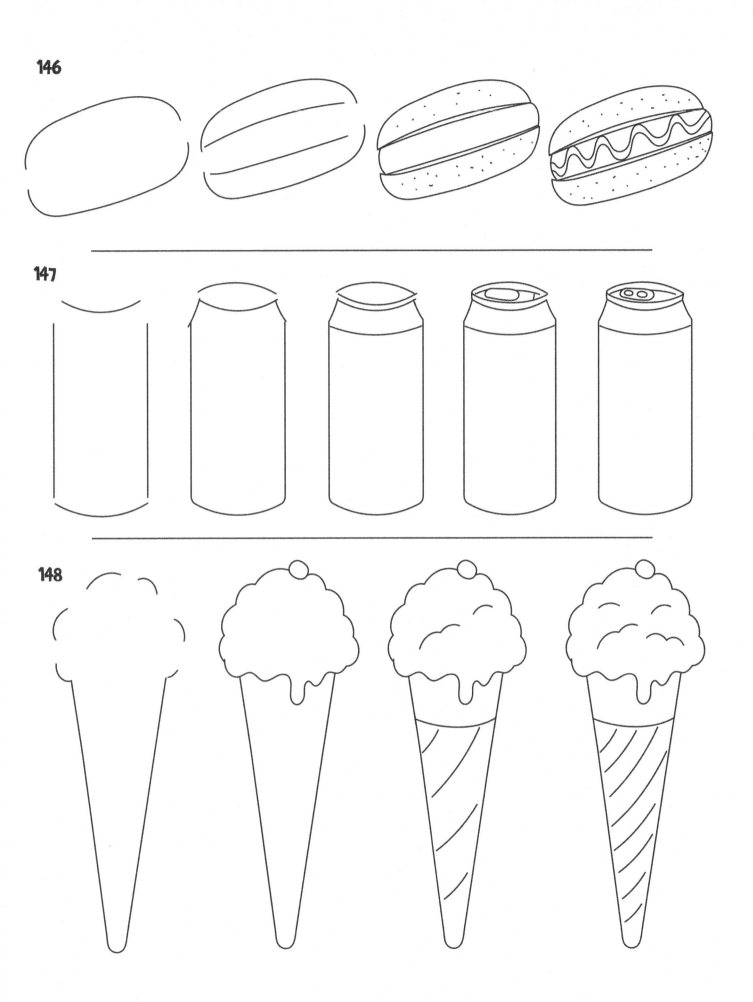

147

148

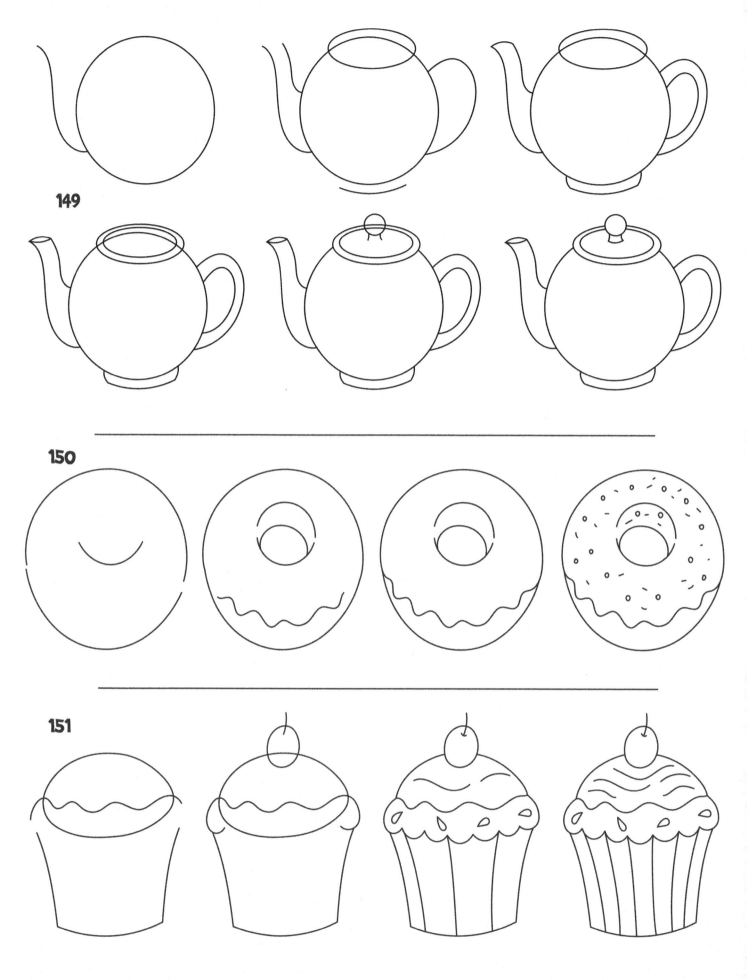

149

150

151

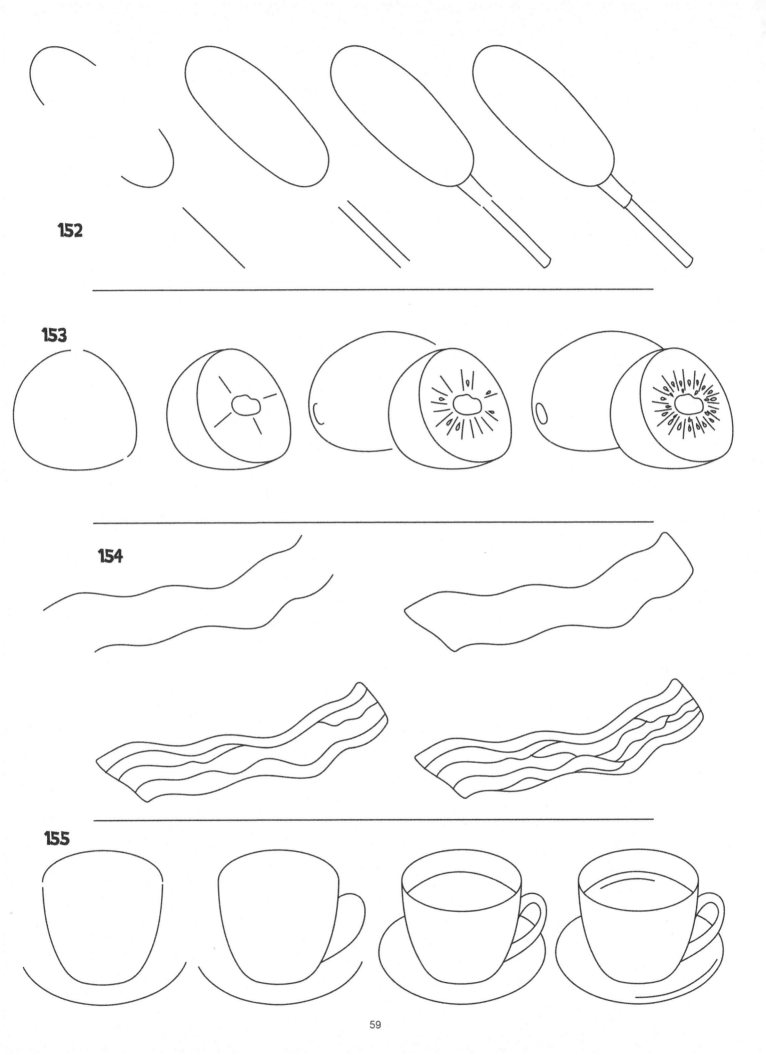

152

153

154

155

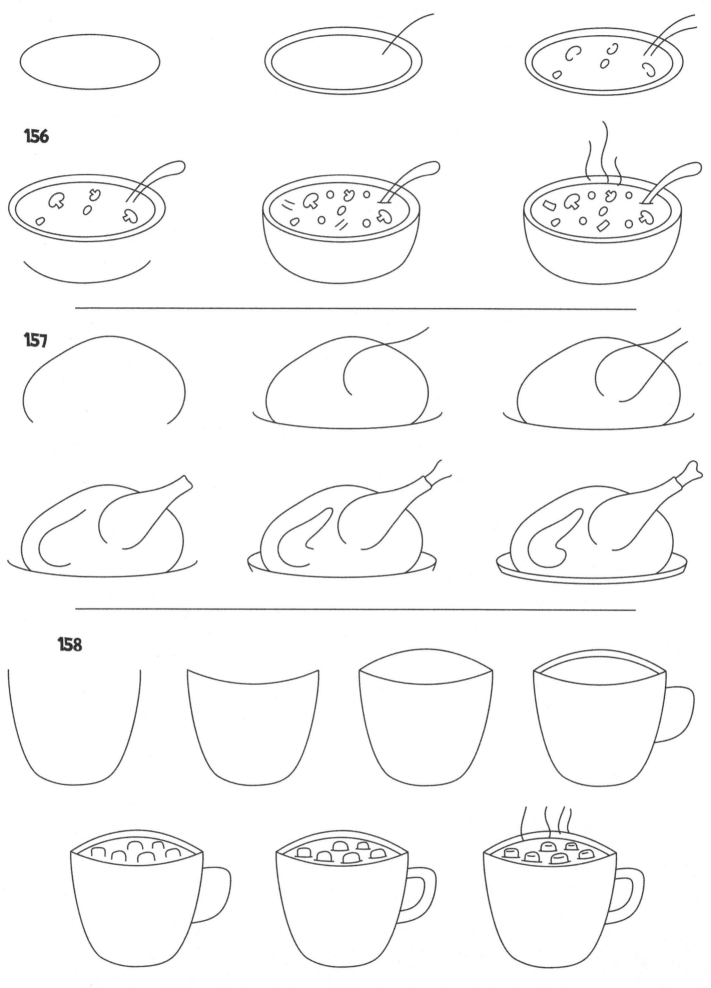

156

157

158

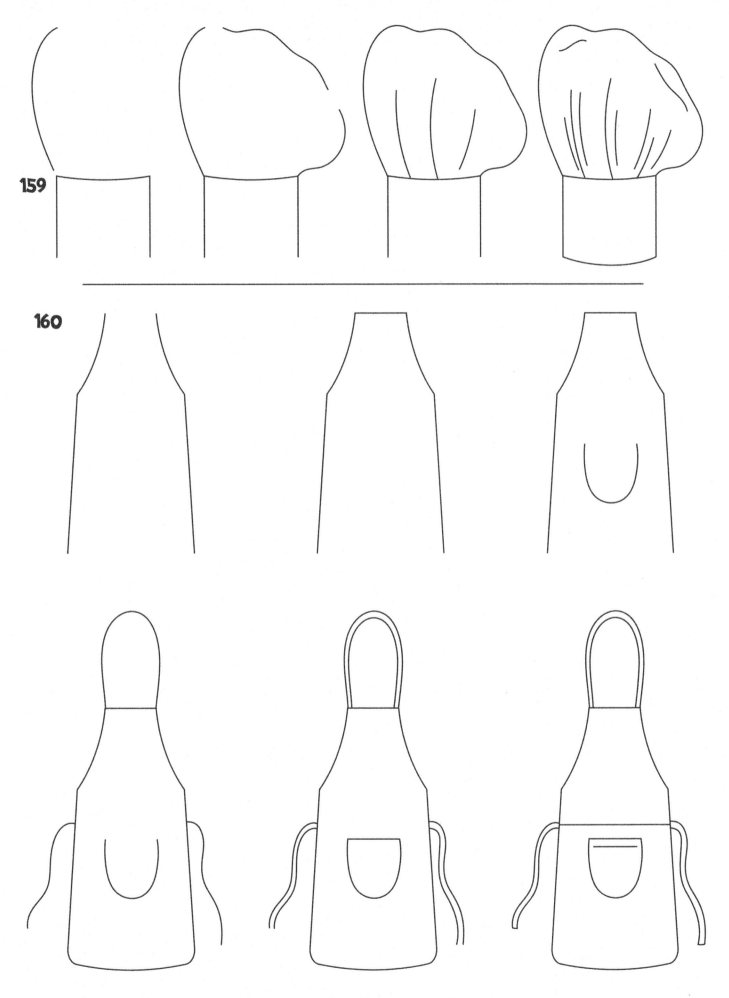

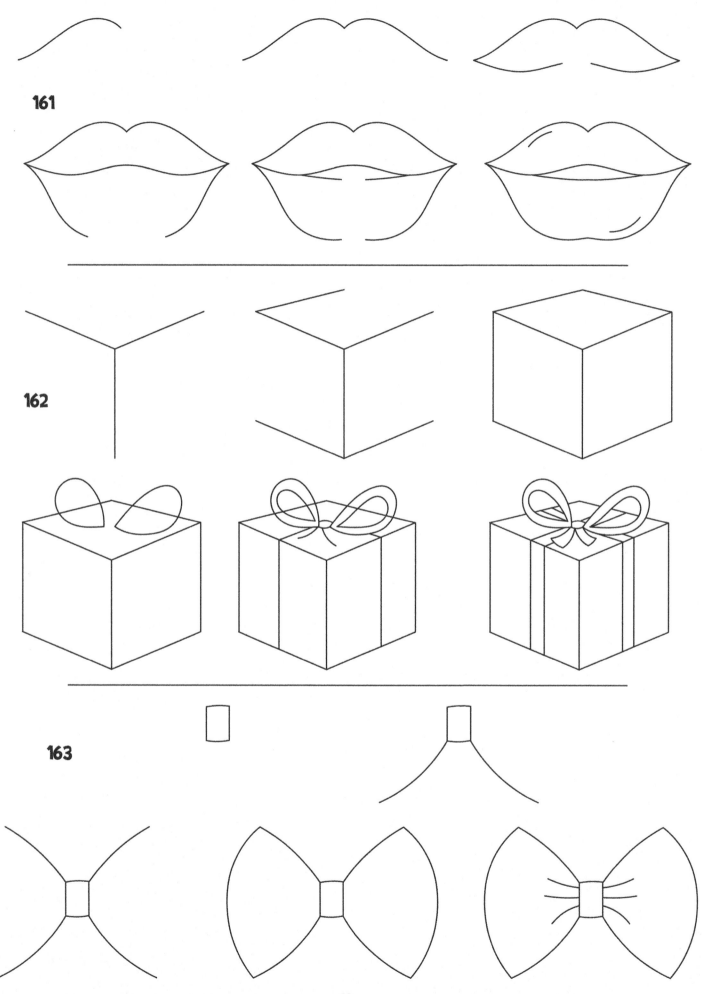

161

162

163

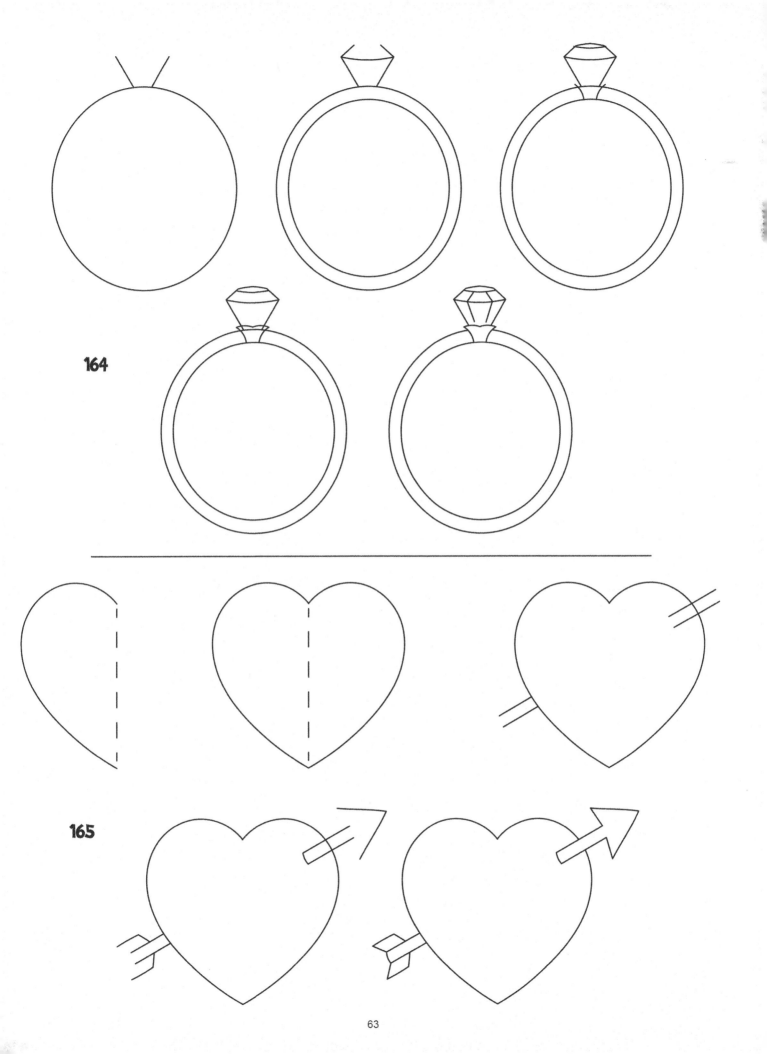

164

165

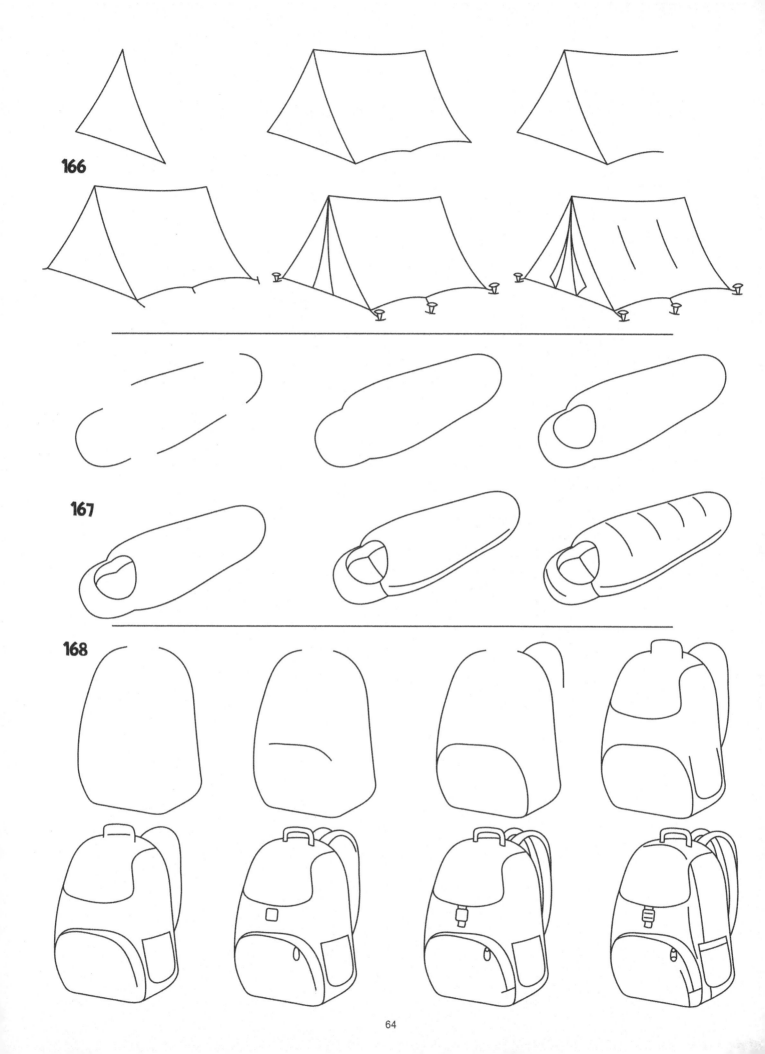

166

167

168

169

170

171

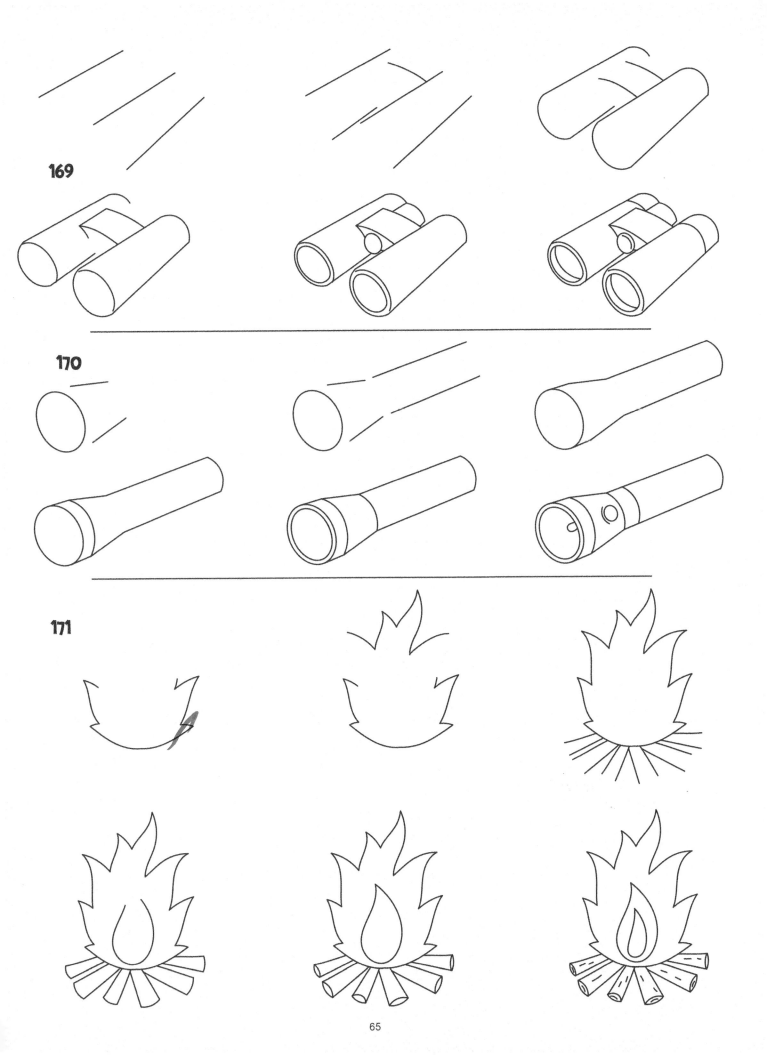

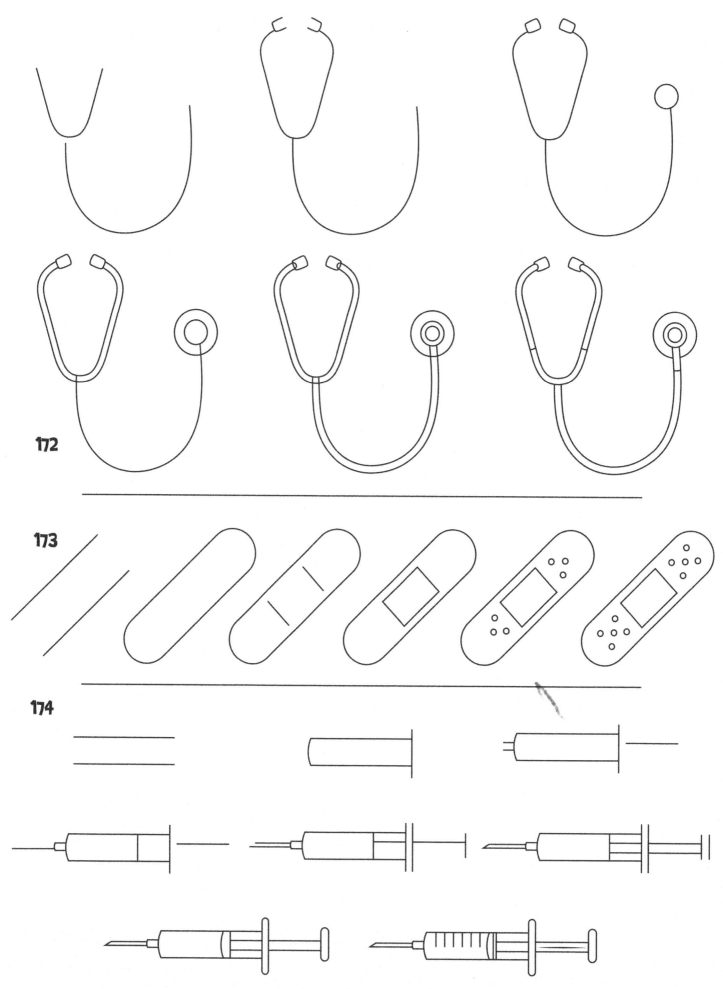

172

173

174

175

176

177

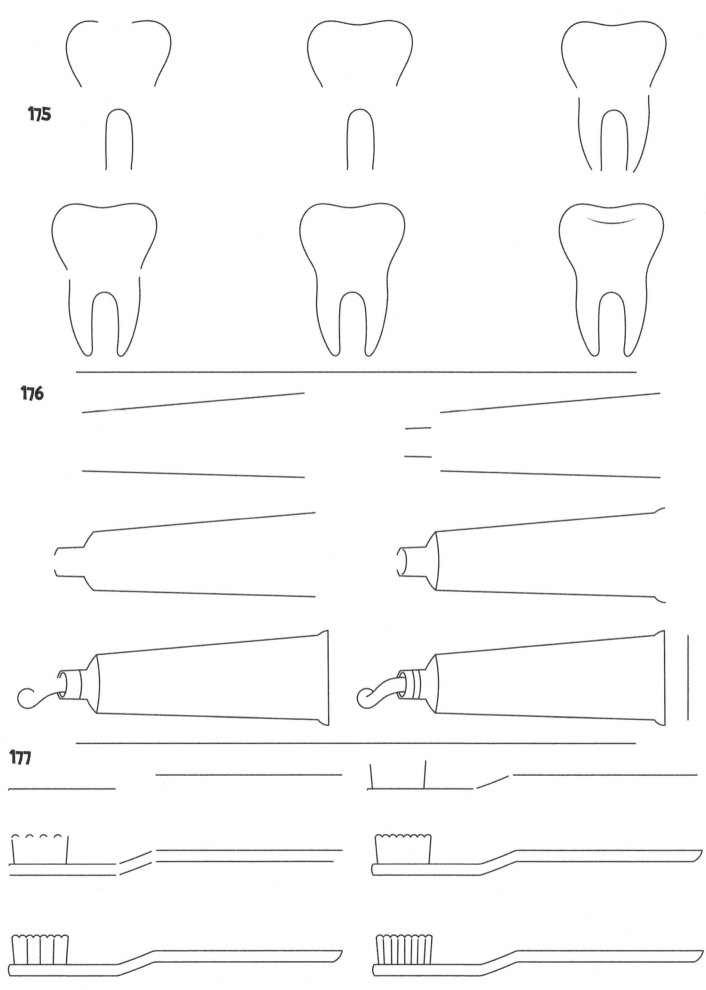

178

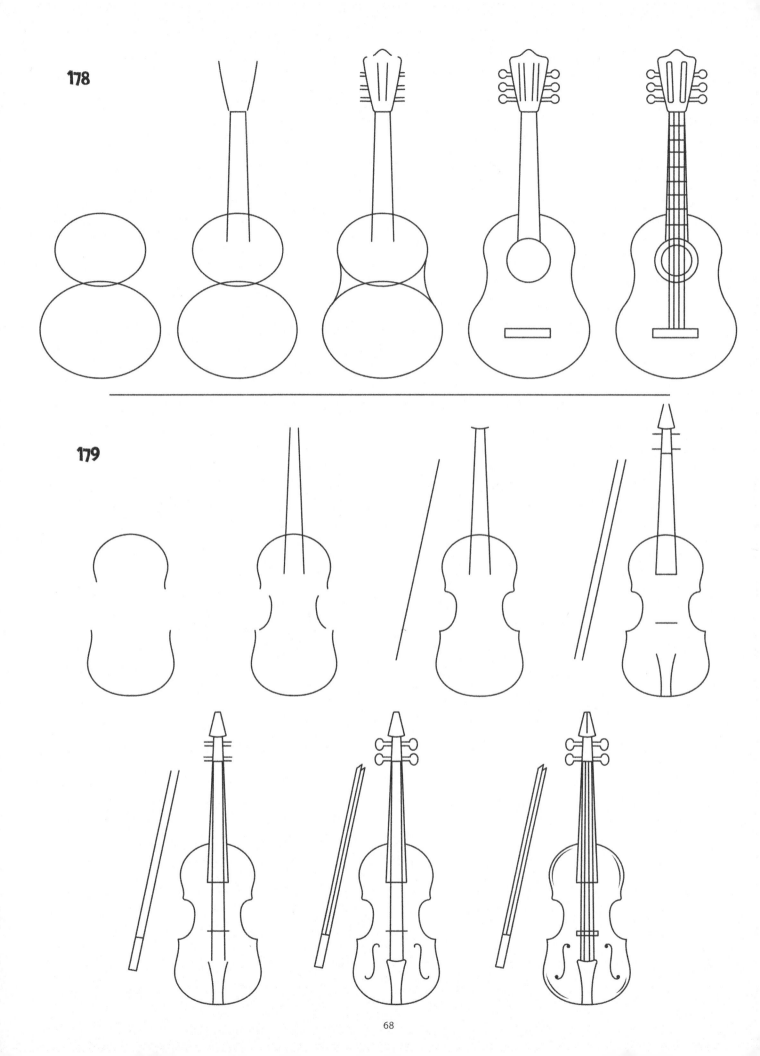

179

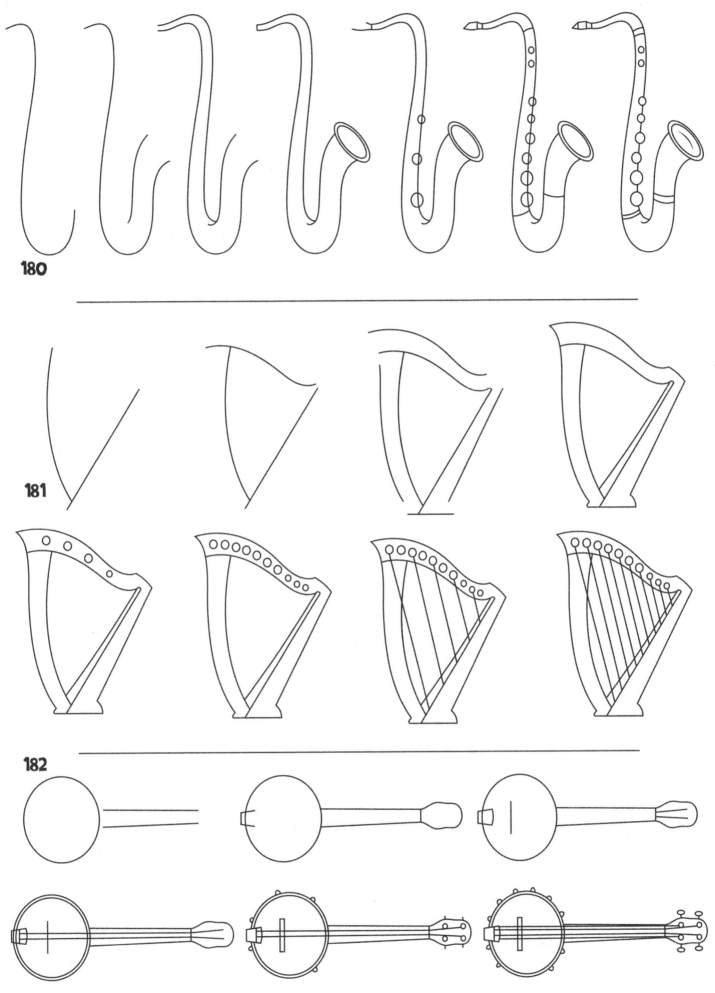

180

181

182

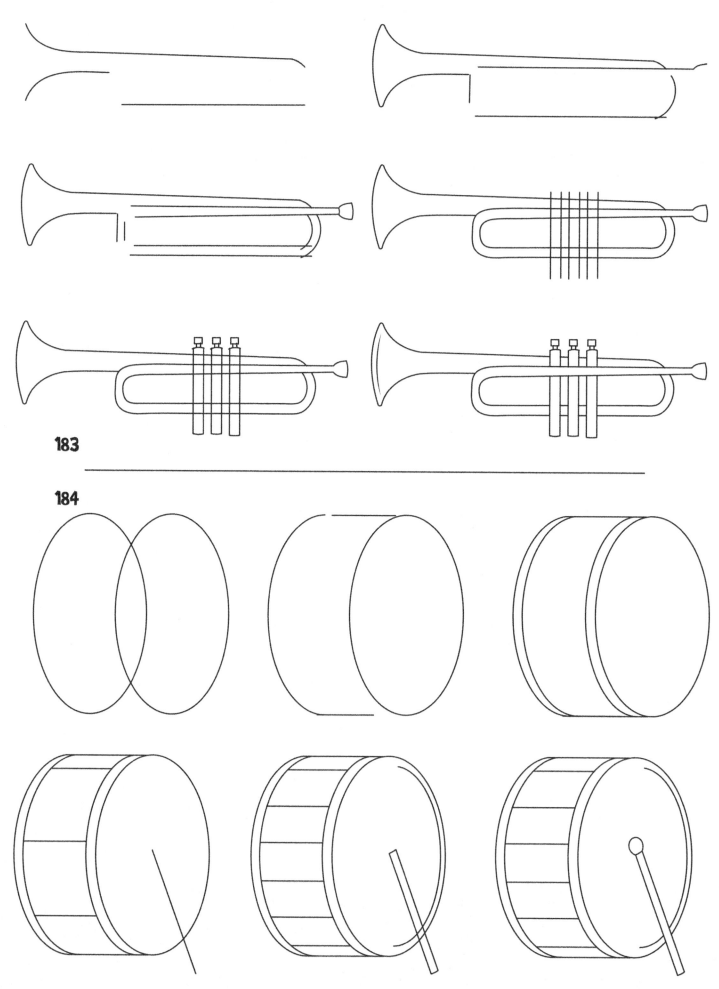

183

184

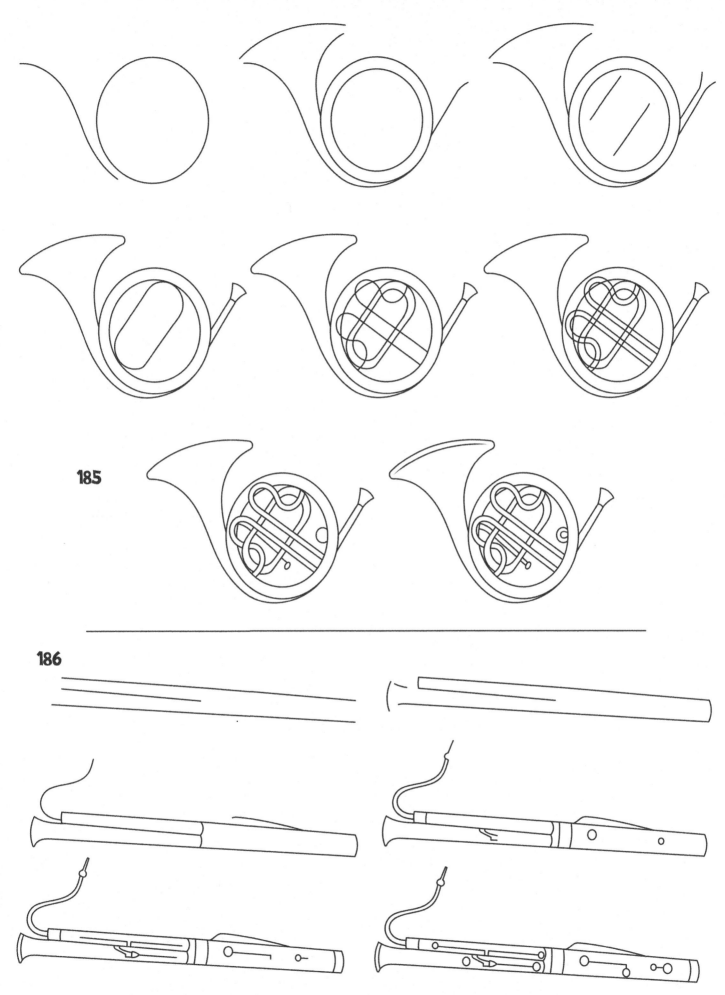

185

186

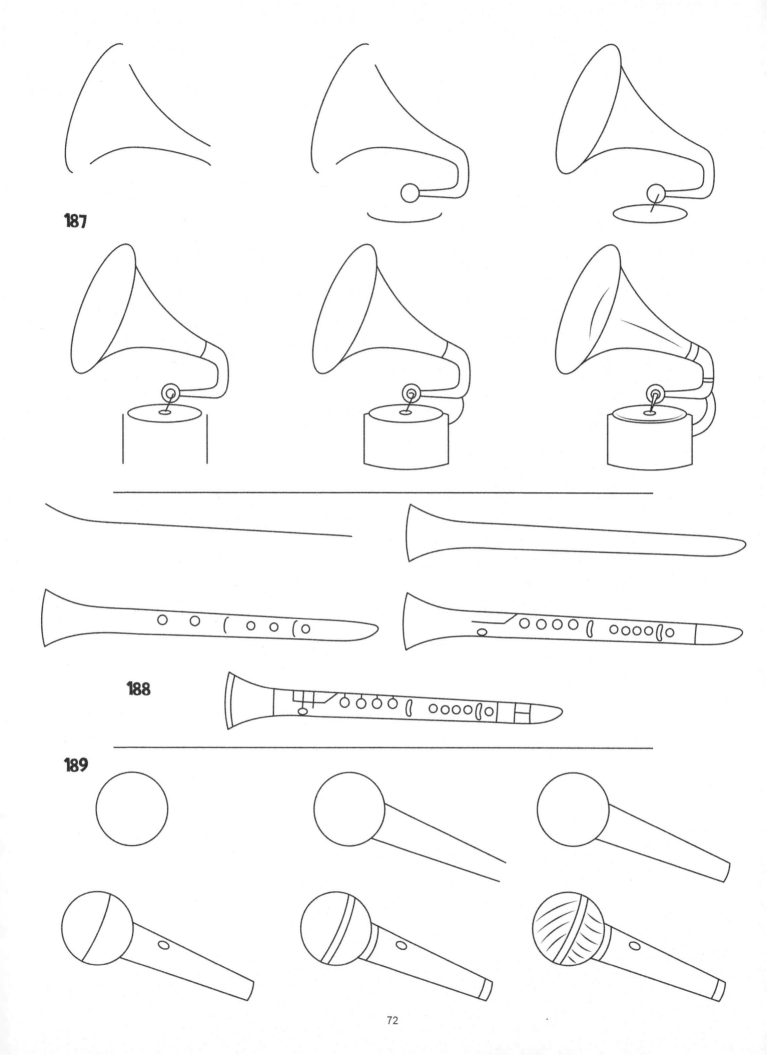

187

188

189

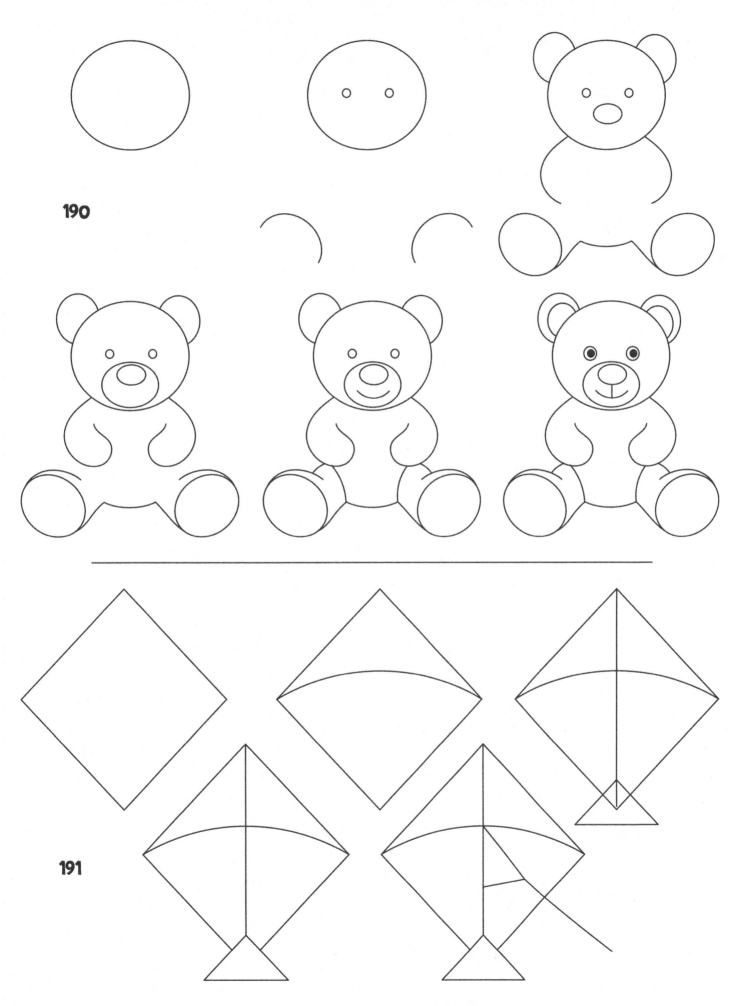

190

191

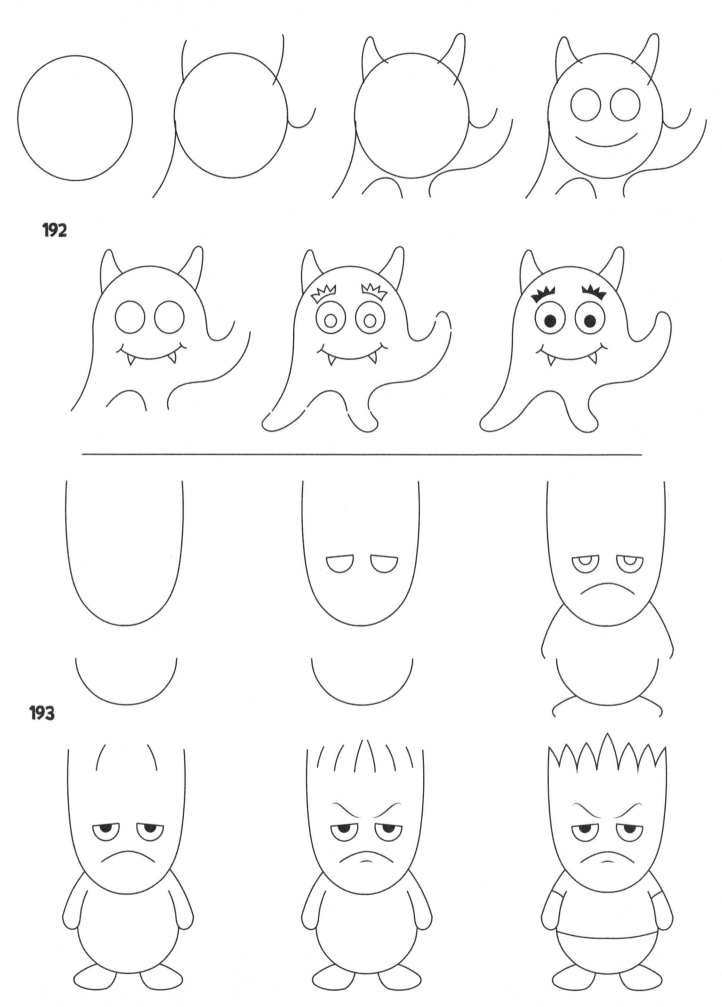

192

193

194

195

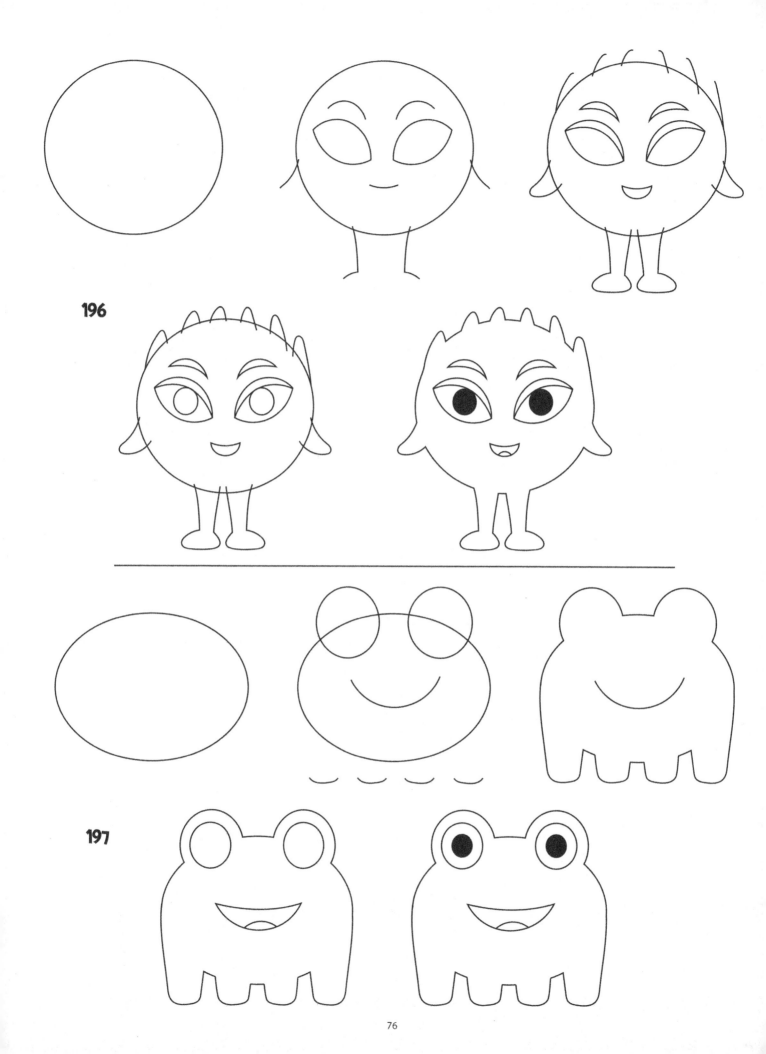

196

197

198

199

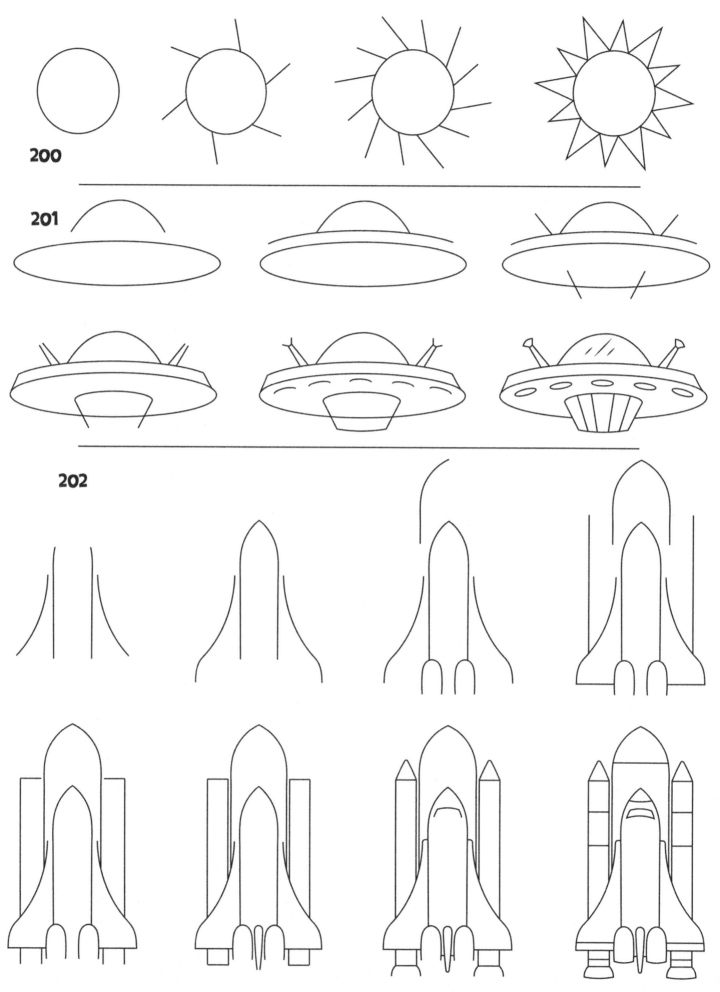

200

201

202

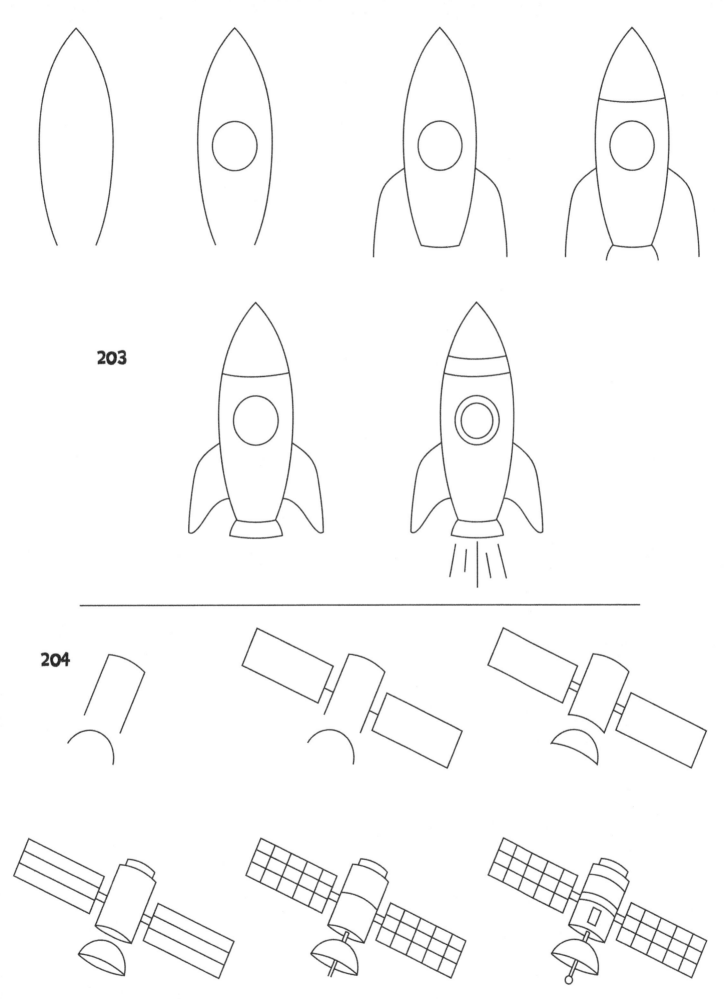

203

204

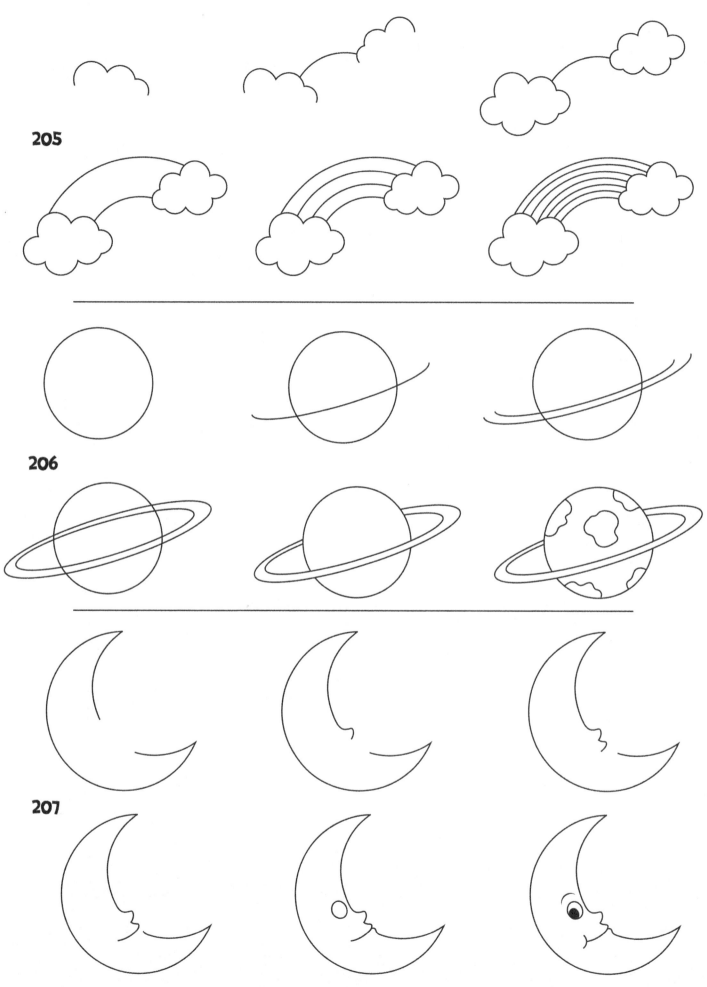

205

206

207

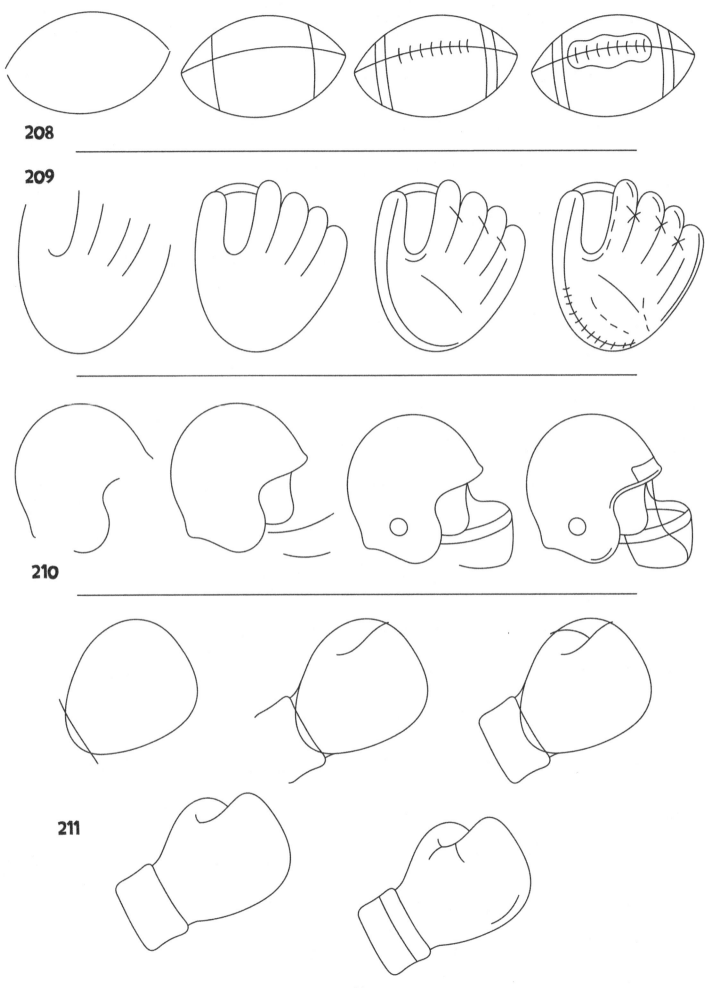

208

209

210

211

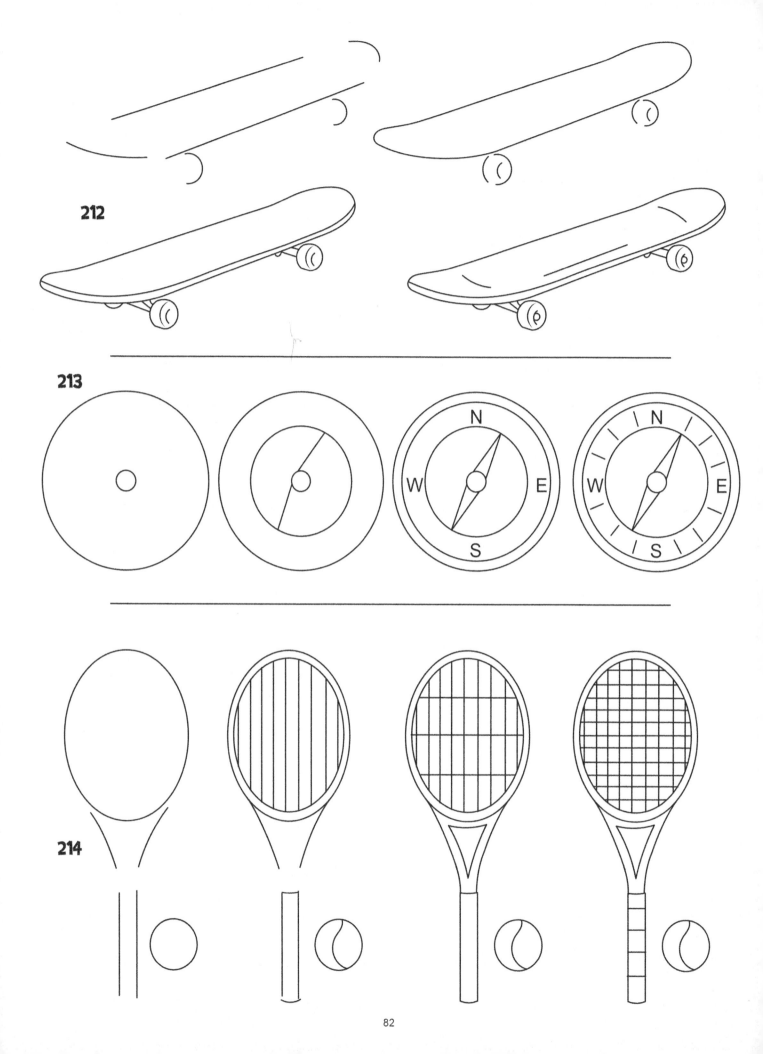

212

213

214

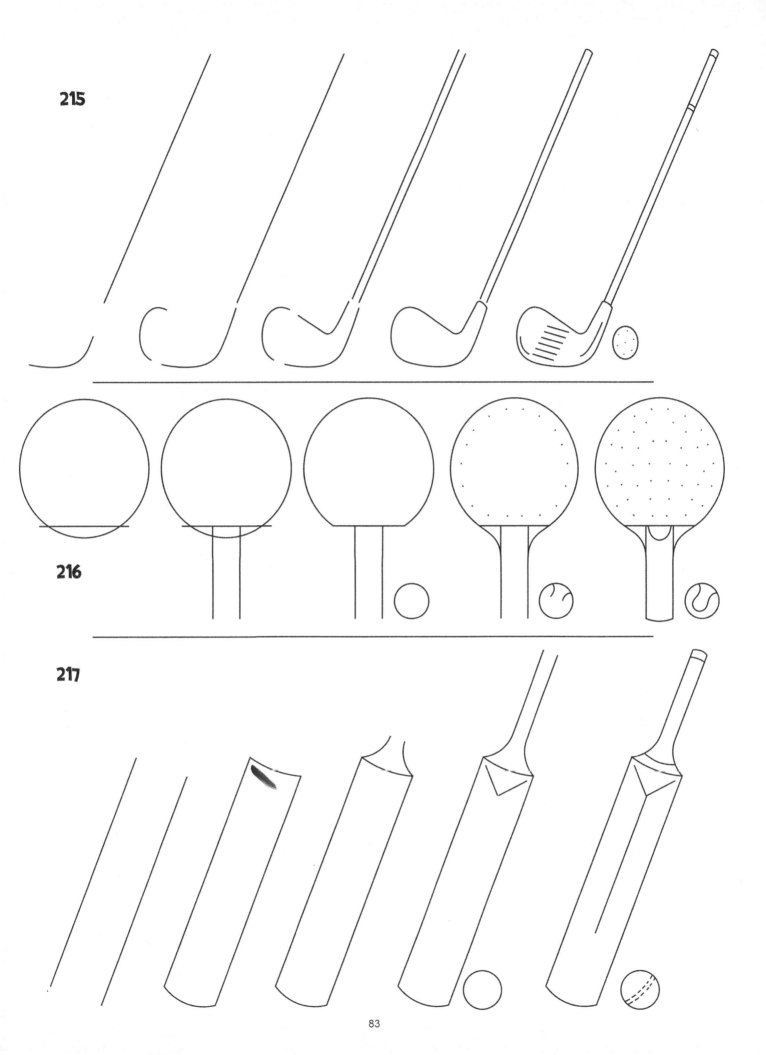

215

216

217

218

219

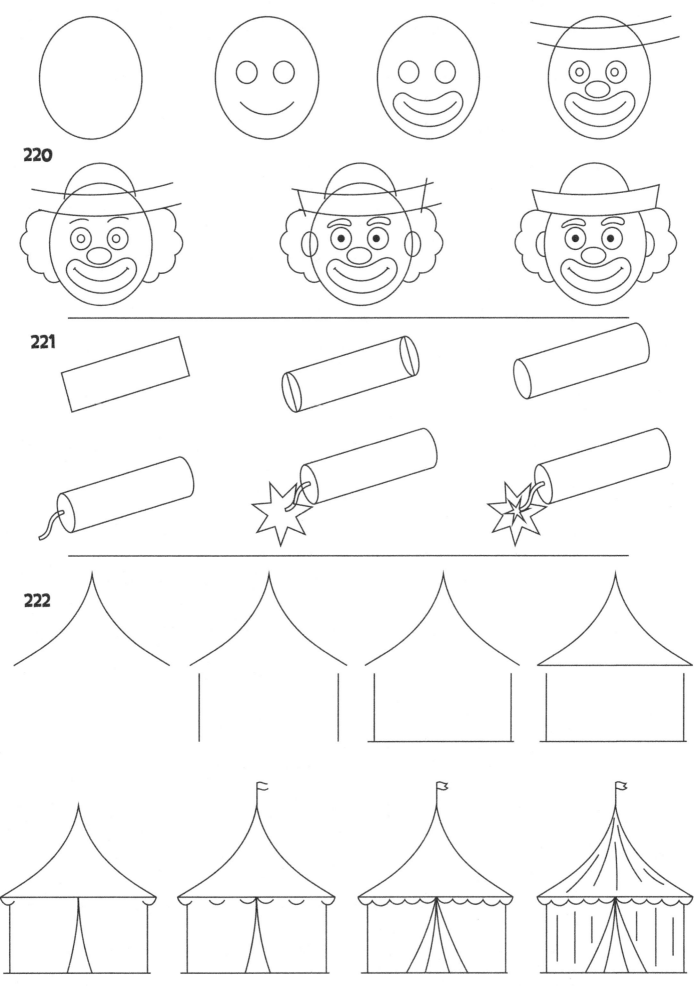

220

221

222

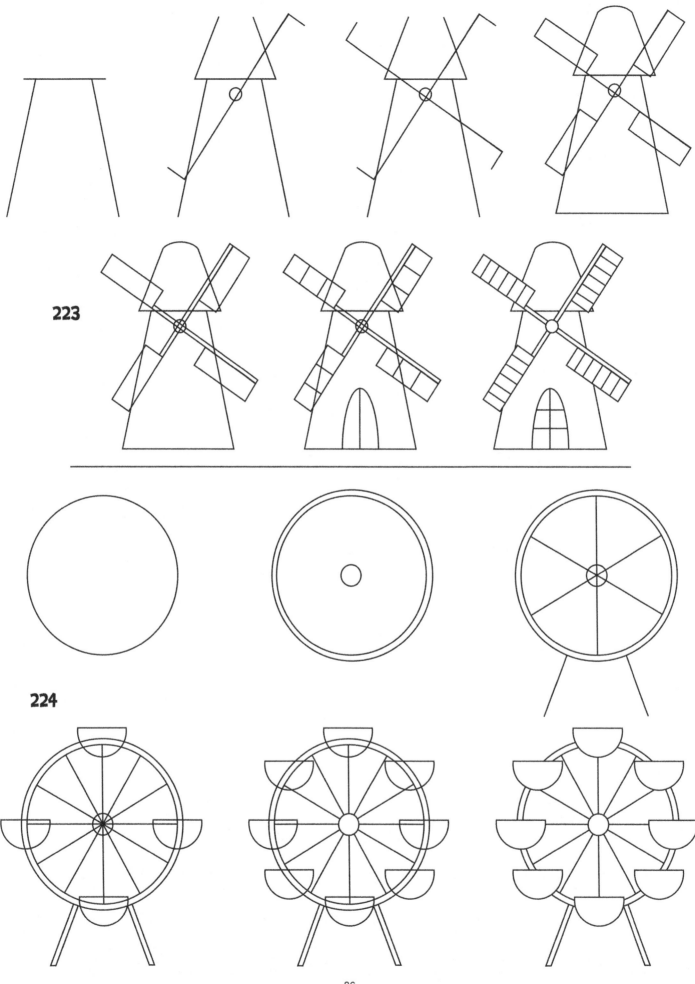

223

224

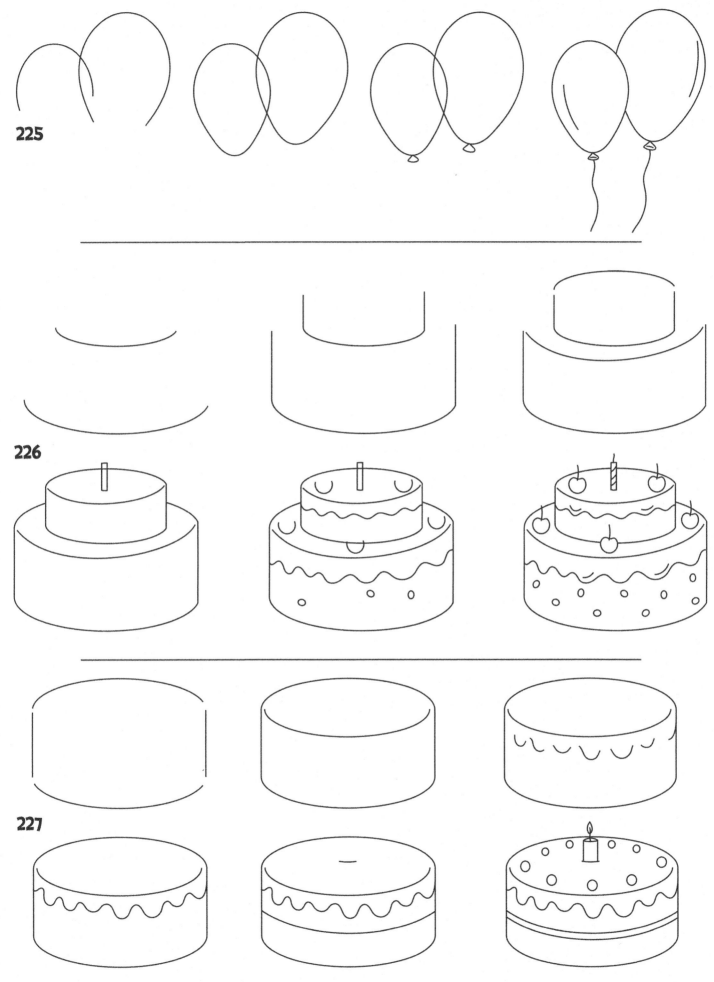

225

226

227

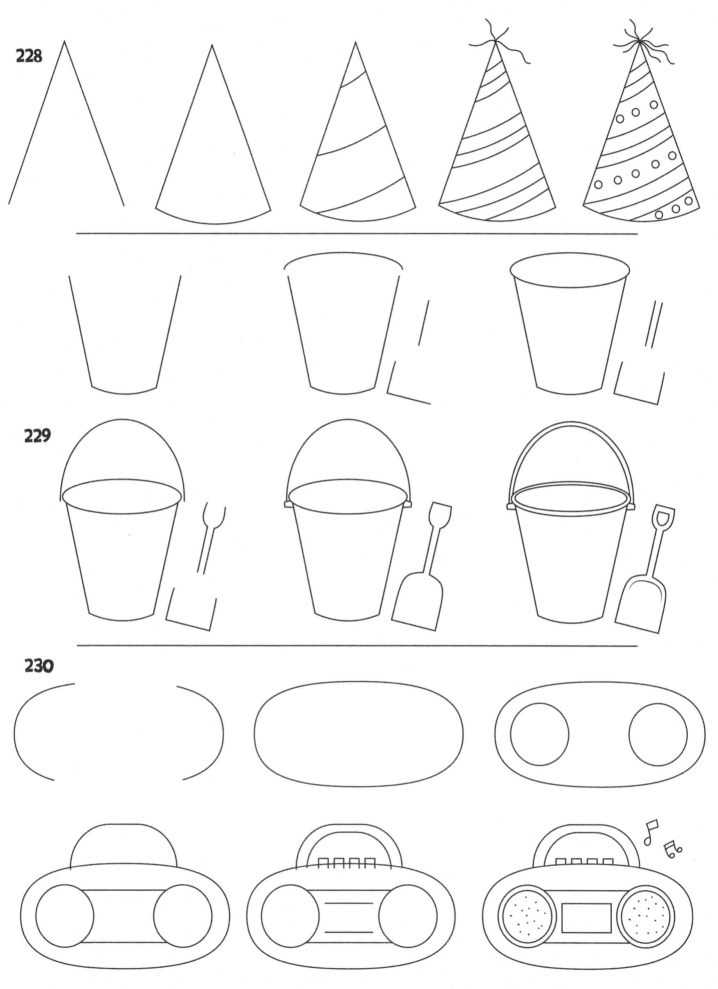

228

229

230

231

232

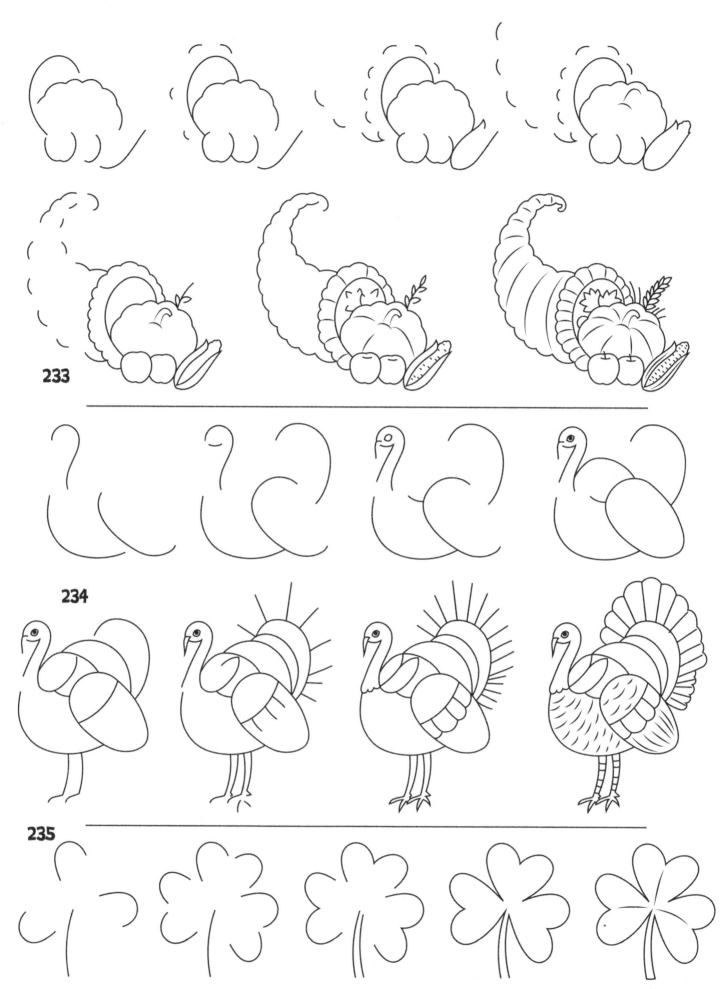

233

234

235

236

237

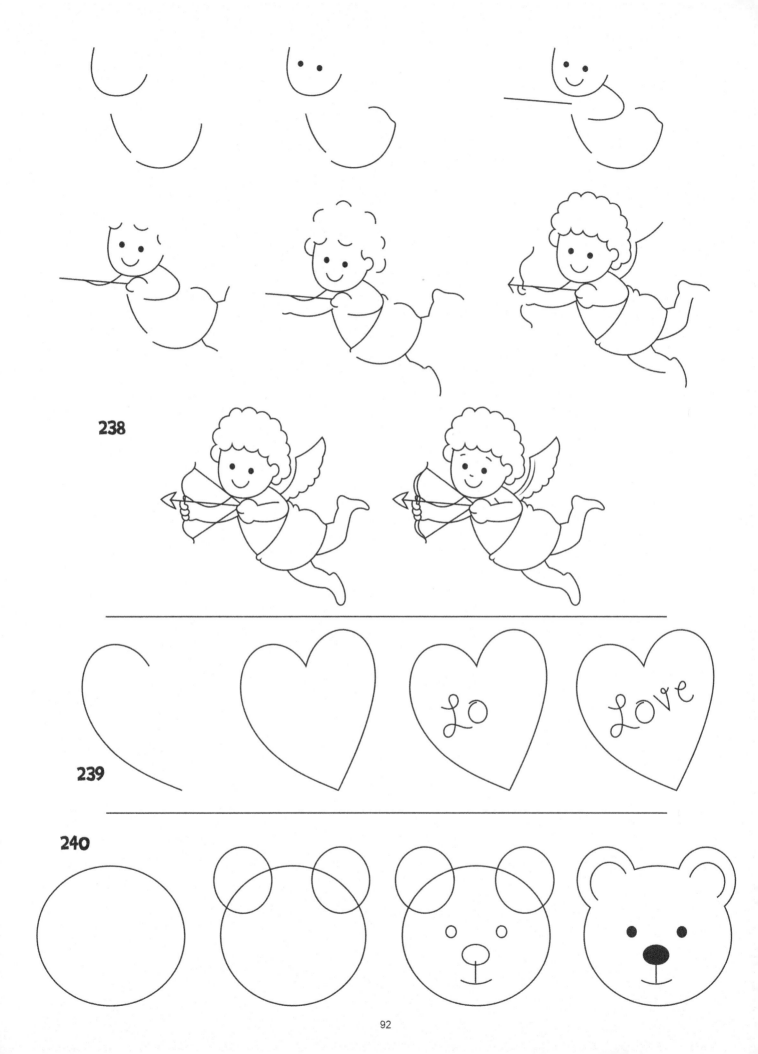

238

239

240

241

242

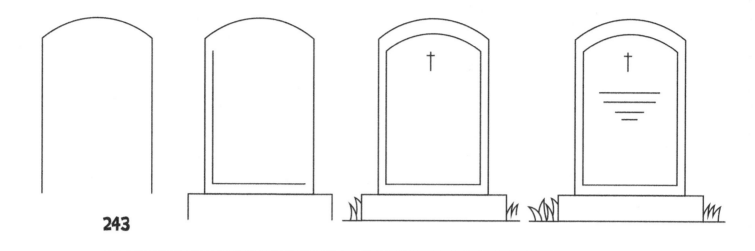

243

244

245

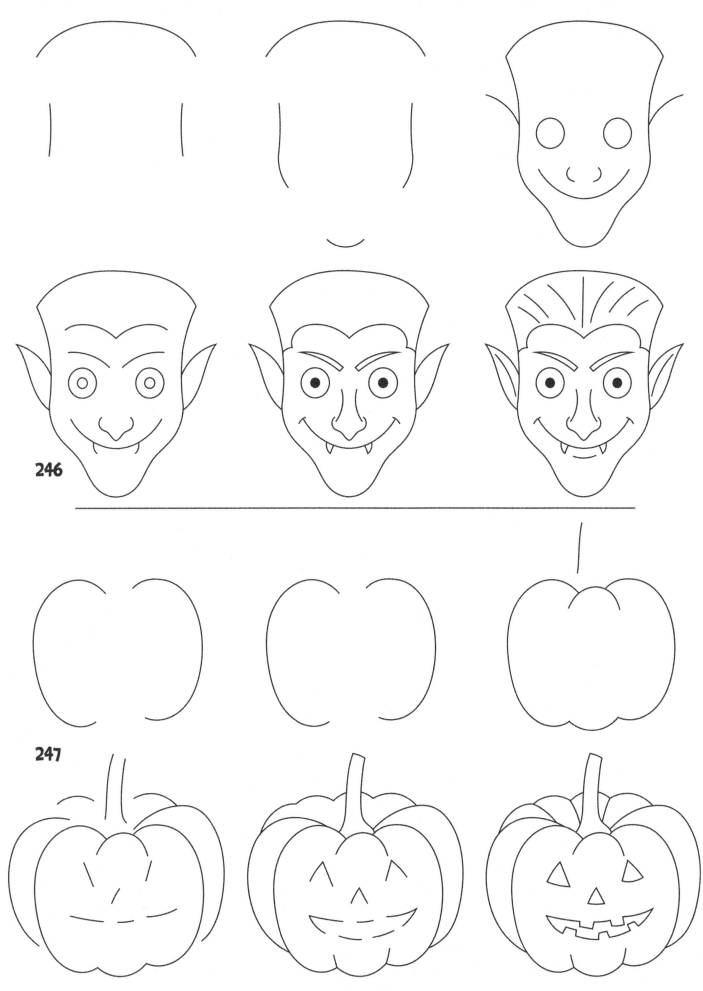

246

247

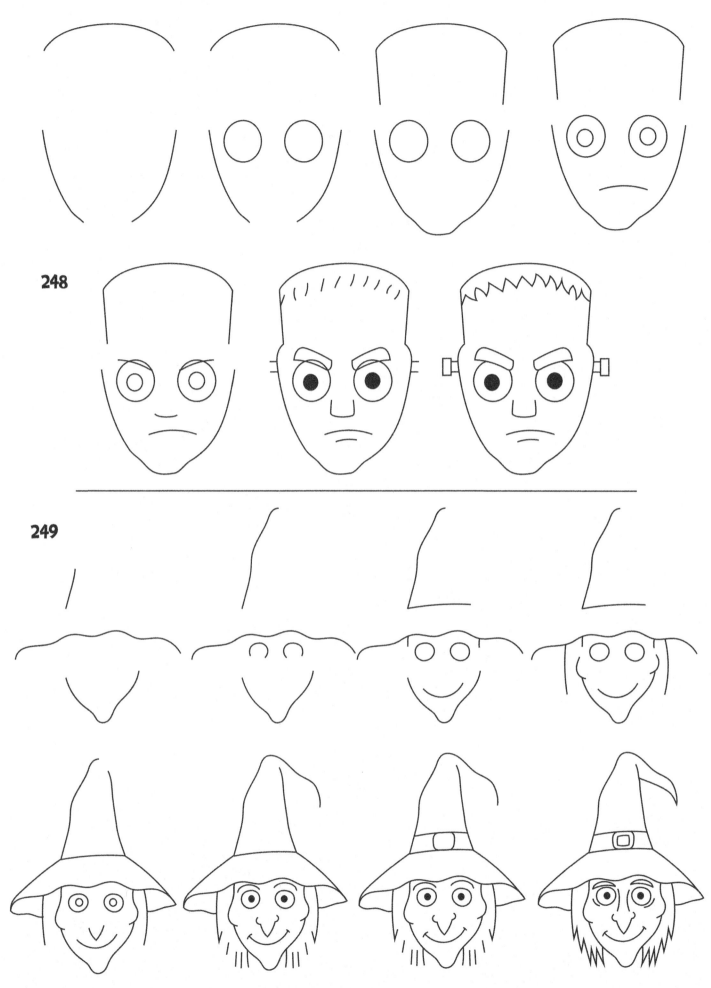

248

249

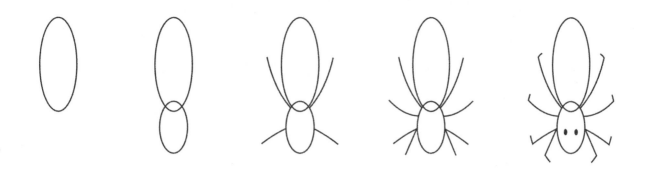

250

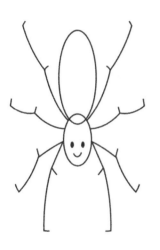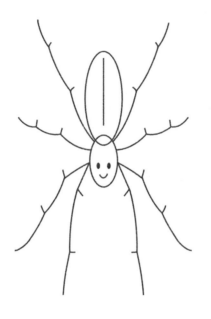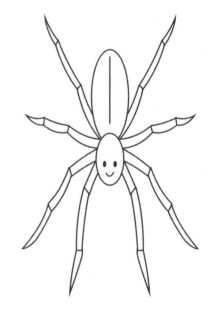

251

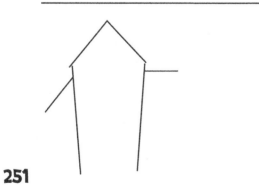

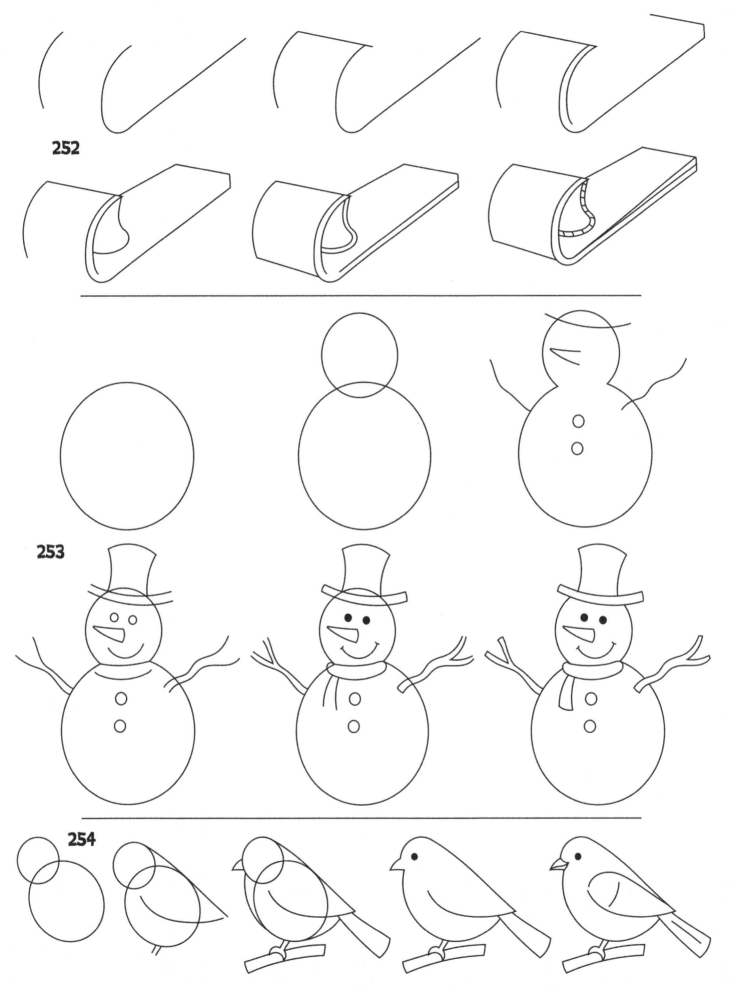

252

253

254

255

256

257

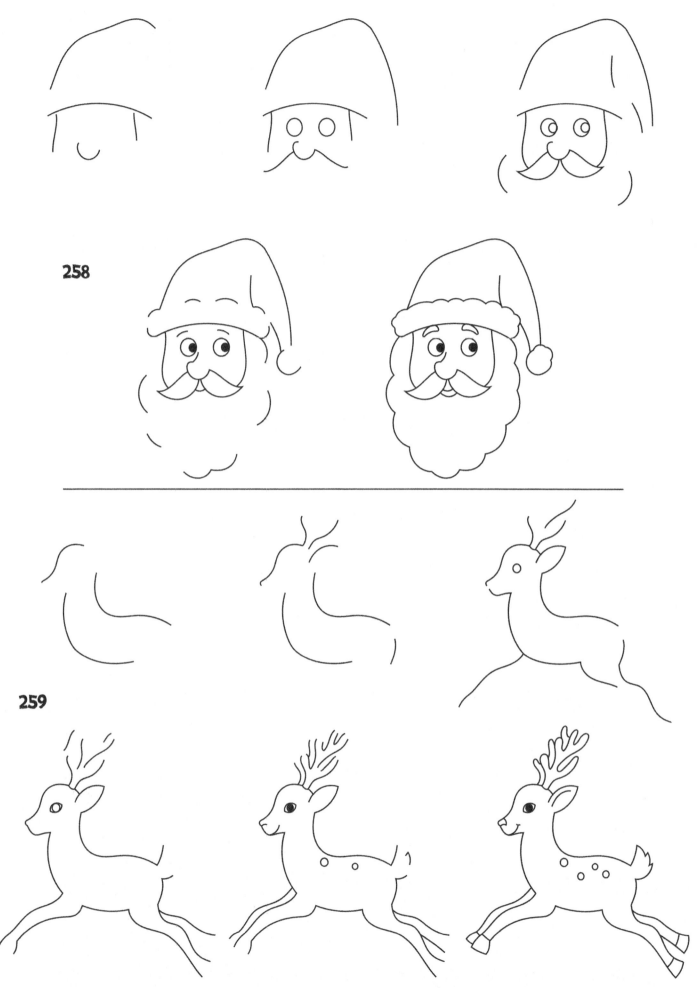

258

259

260

261

262

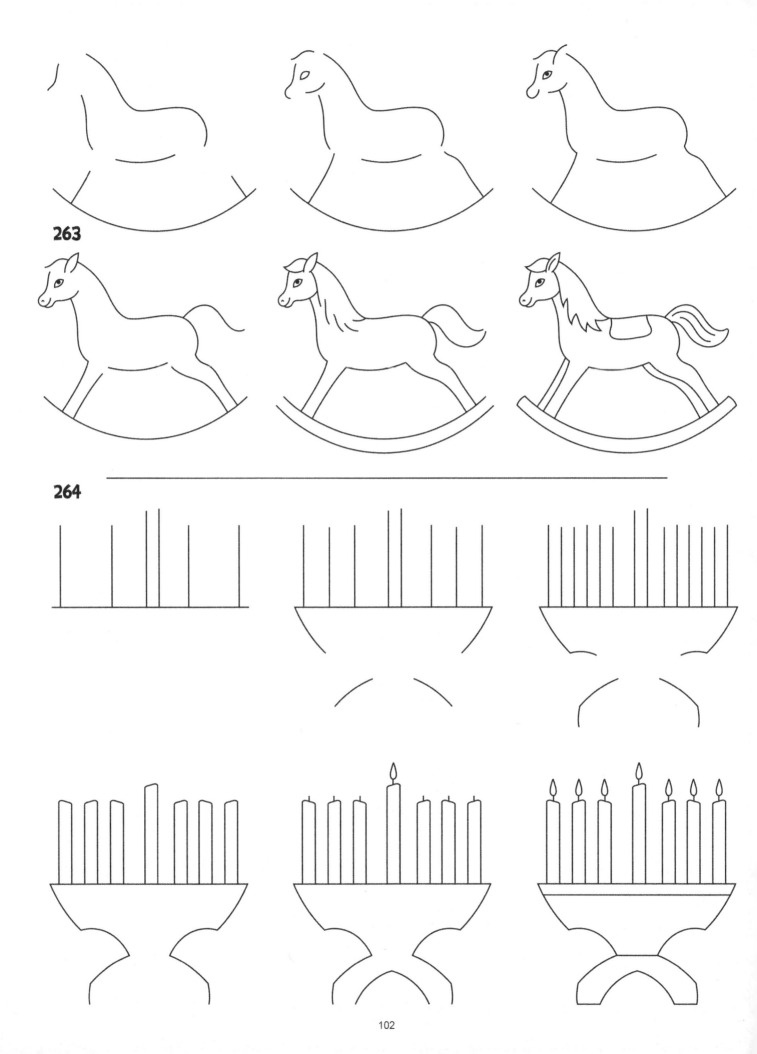

263

264

265

266

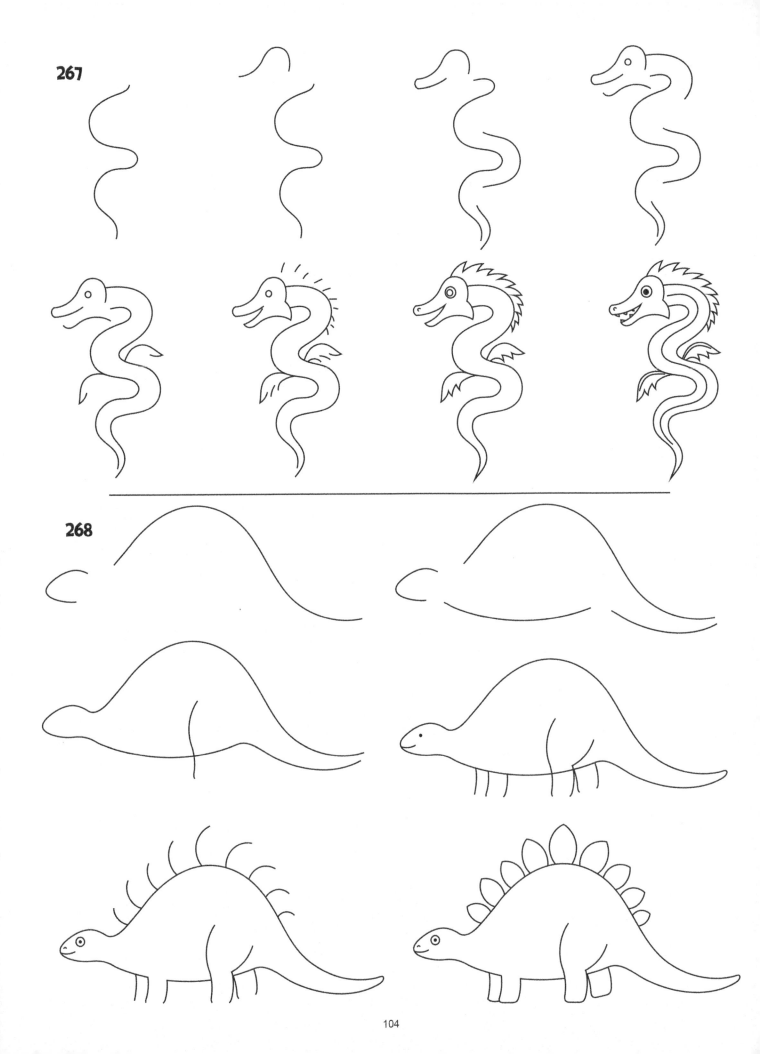

267

268

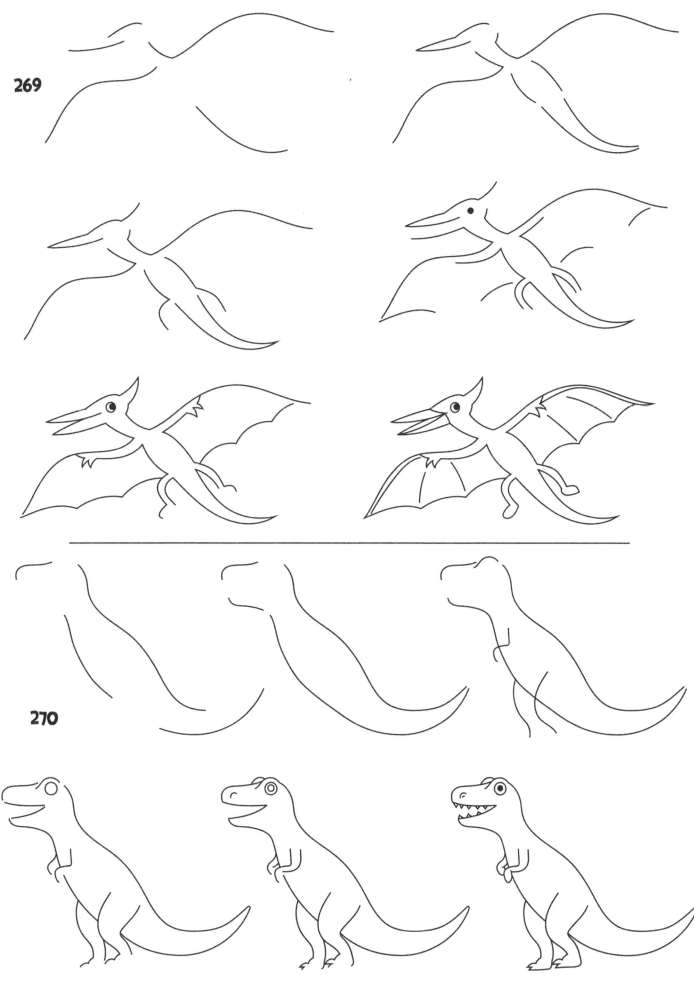

269

270

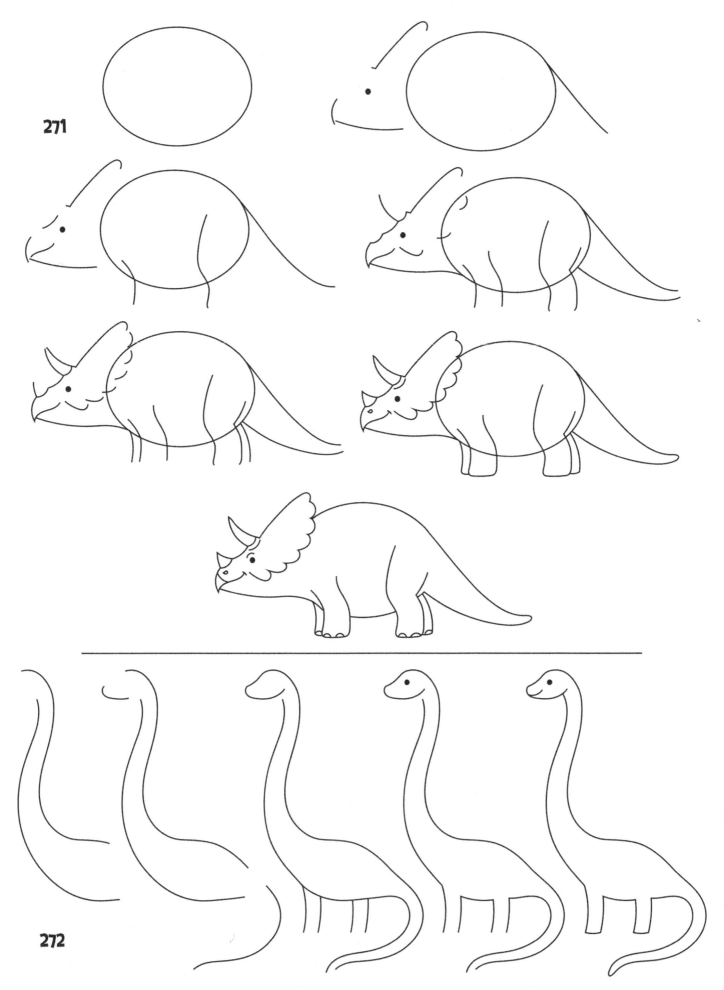

271

272

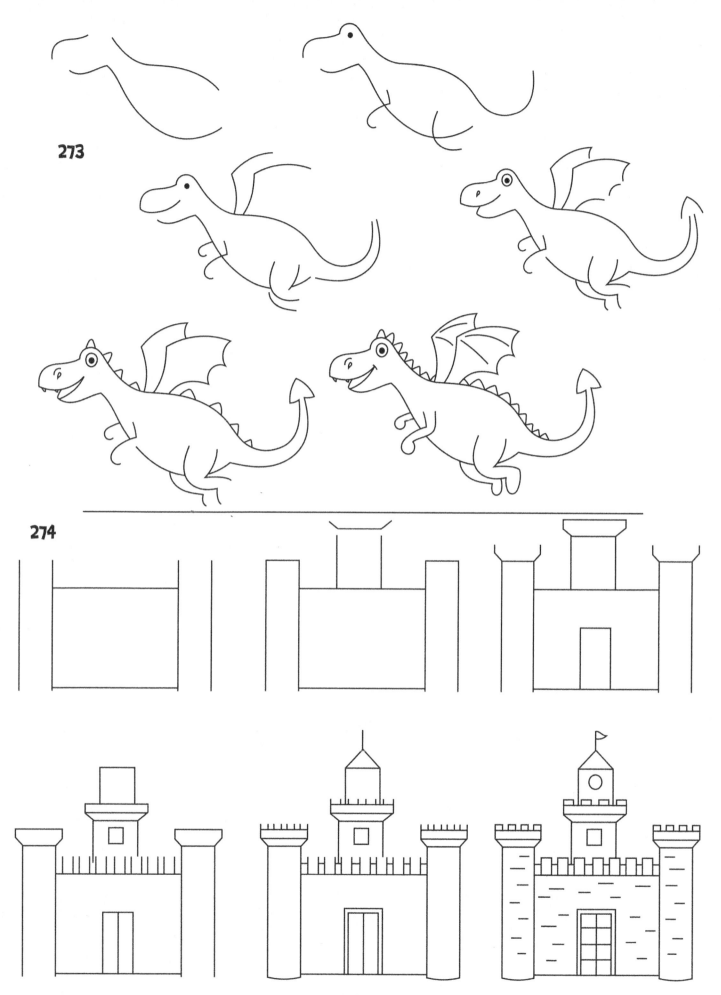

273

274

275

276

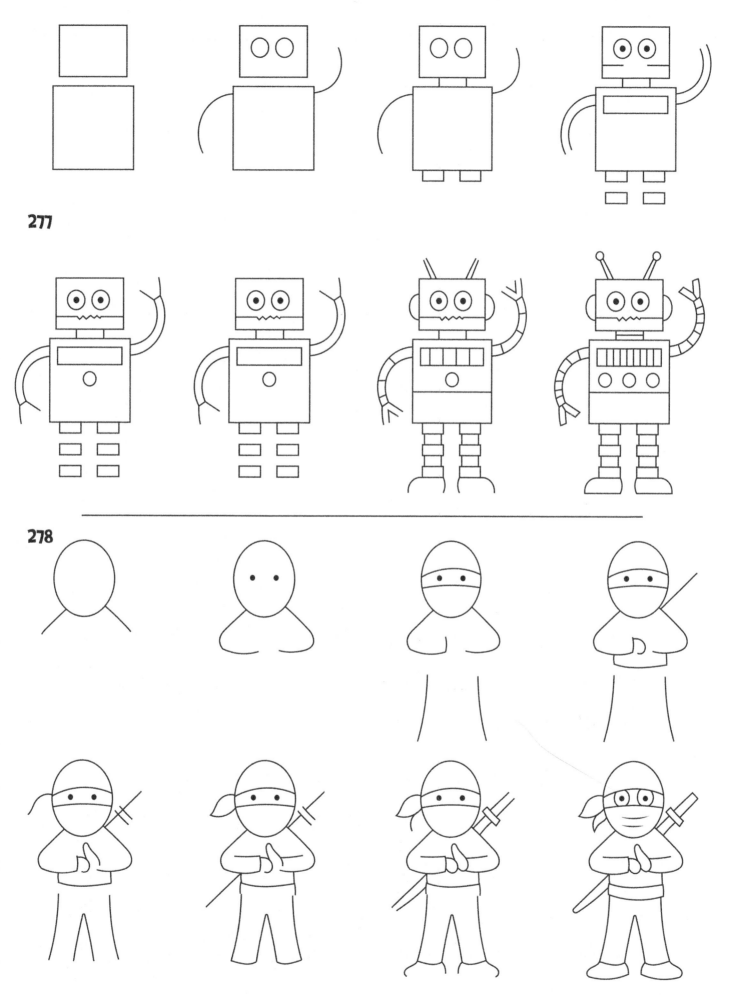

277

278

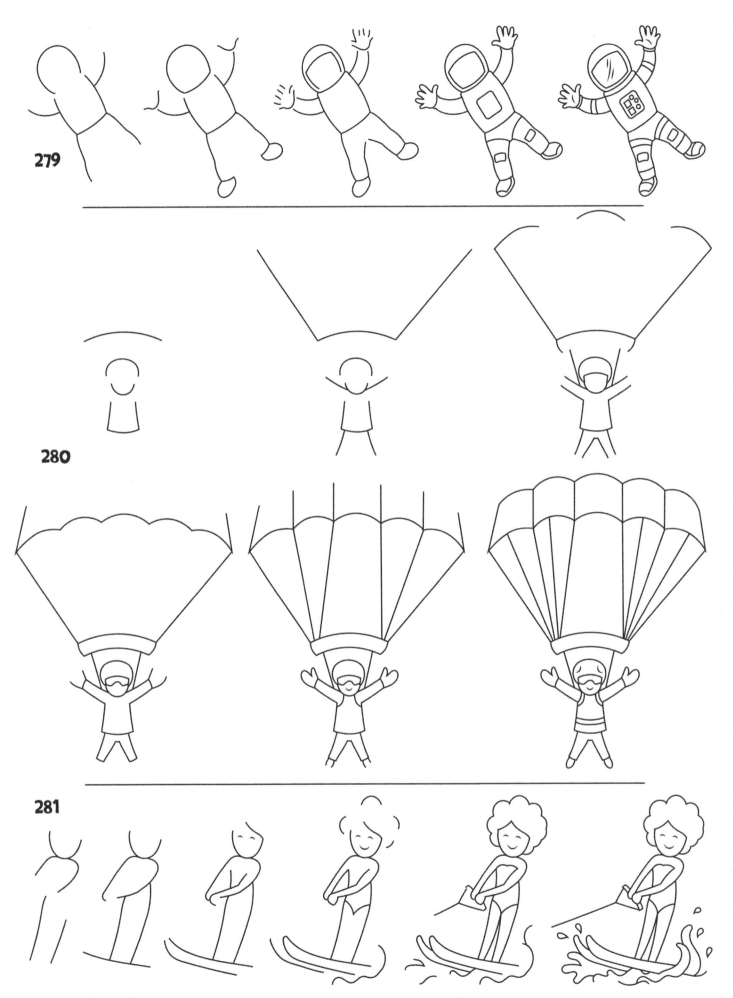

279

280

281

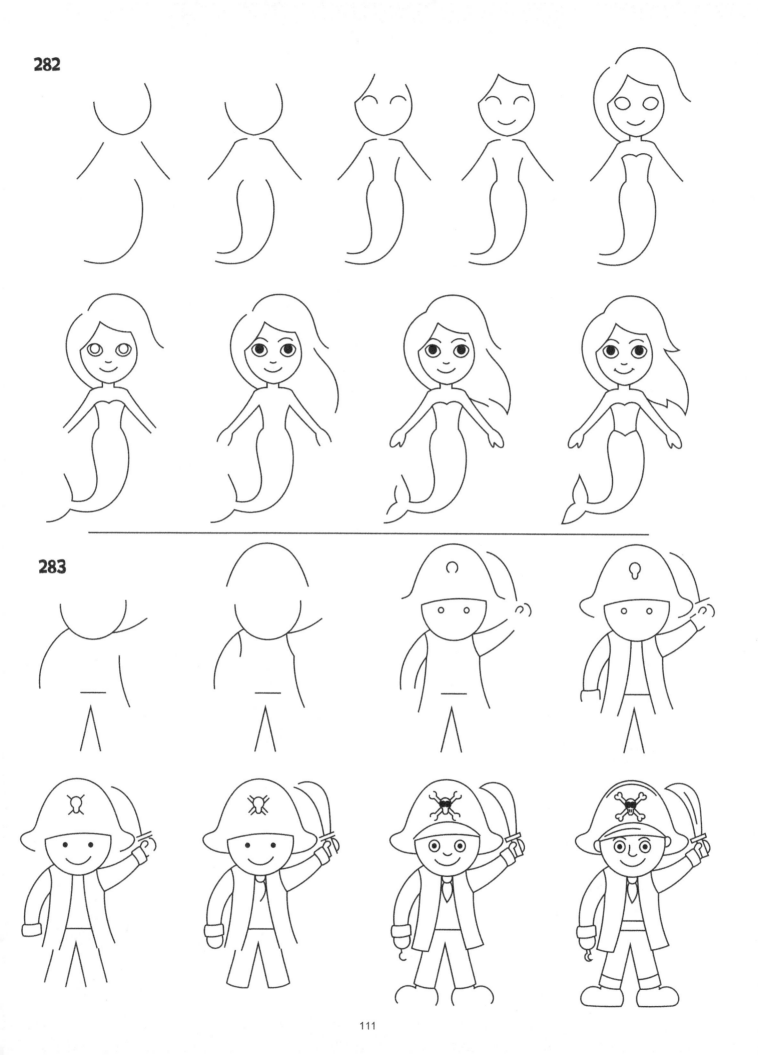

282

283

284

285

286

287

288

289

290

291

292

293

294

295

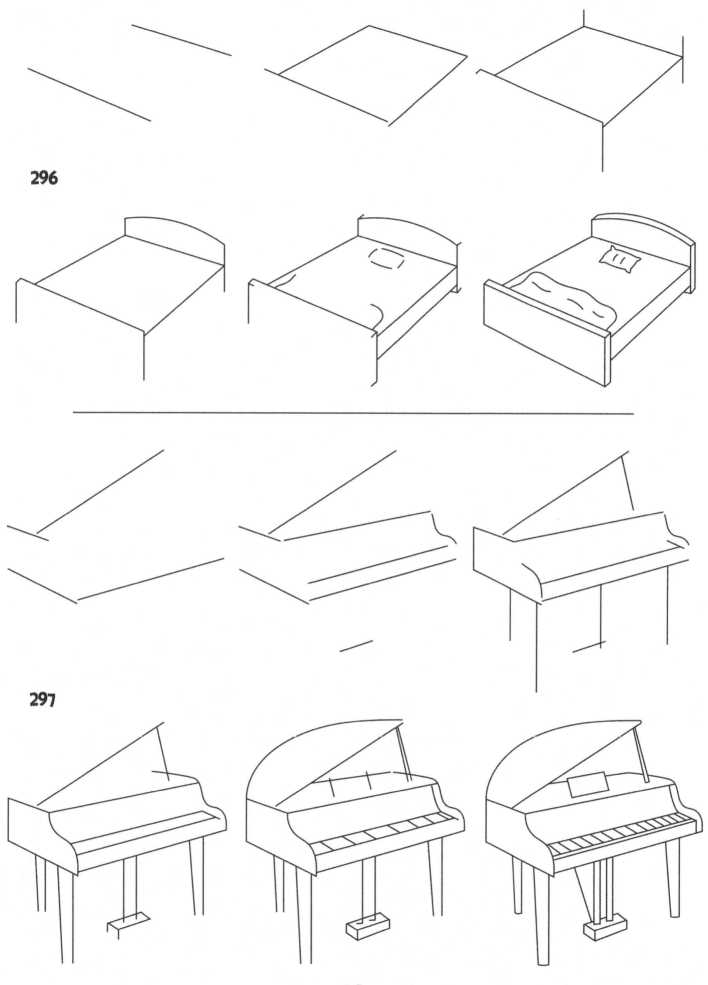

296

297

298

299

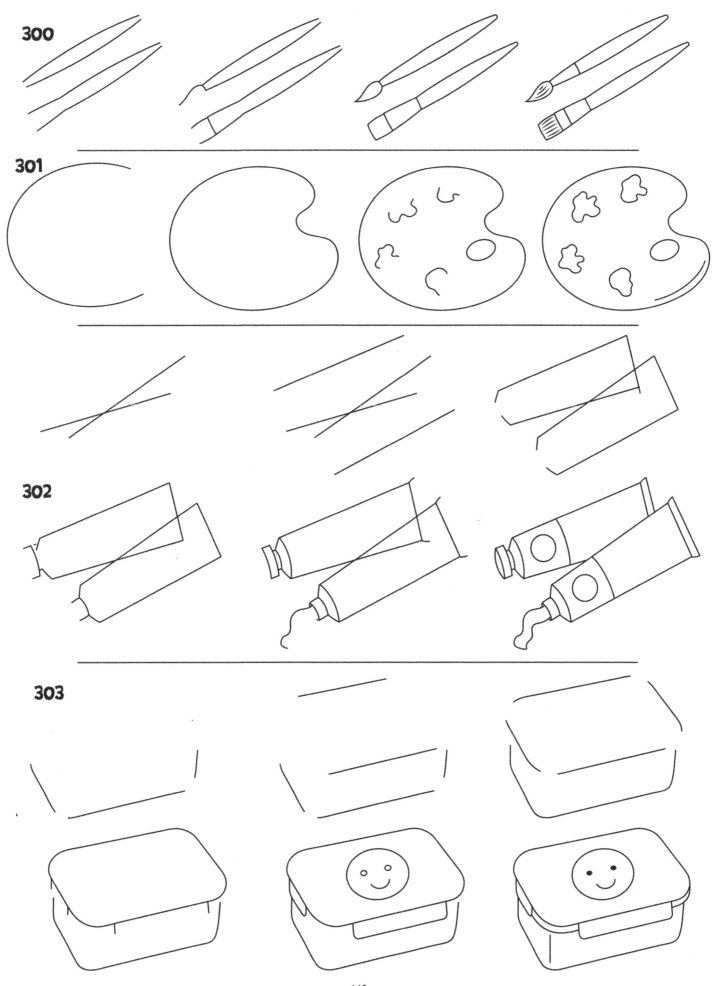

300

301

302

303

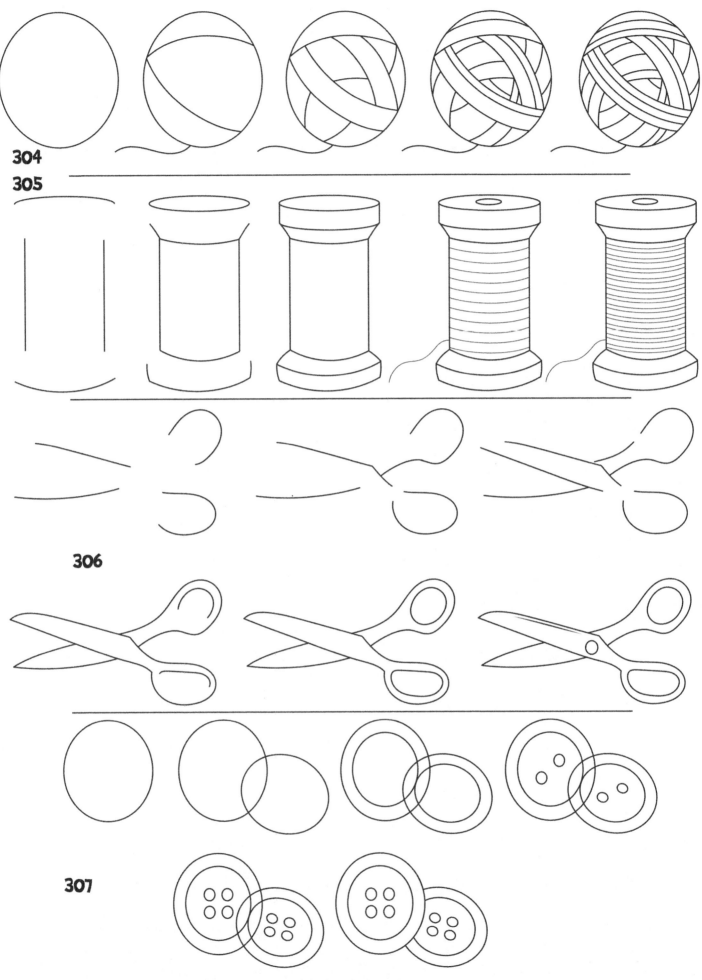

304

305

306

307

120

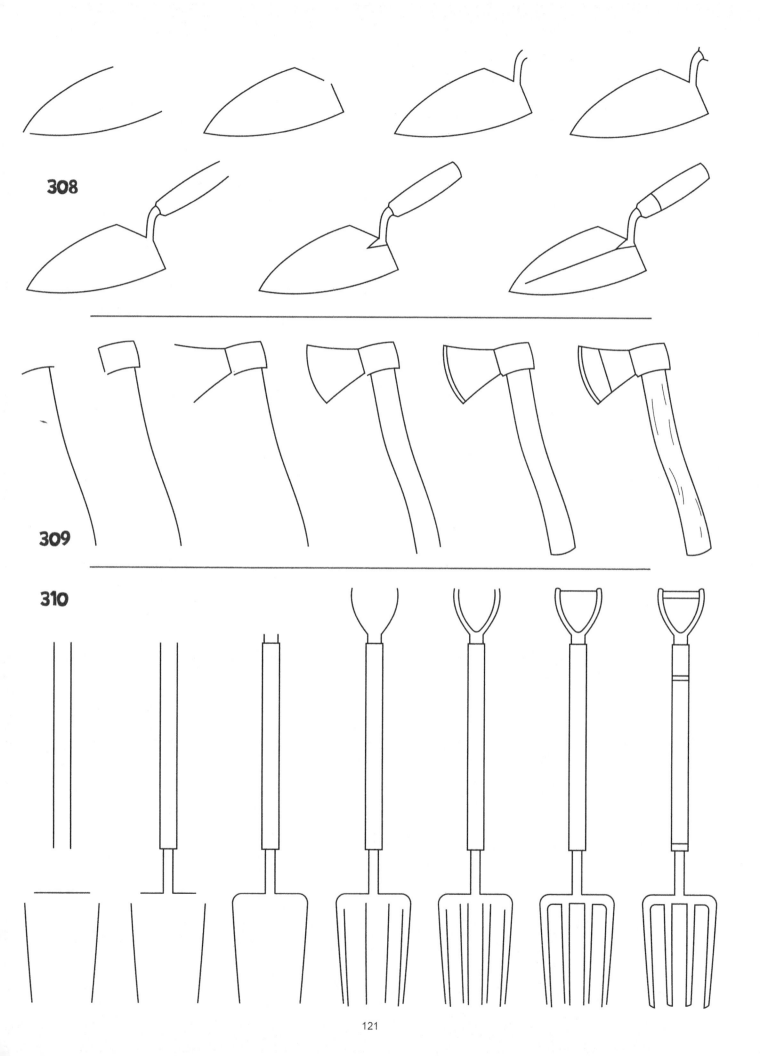

308

309

310

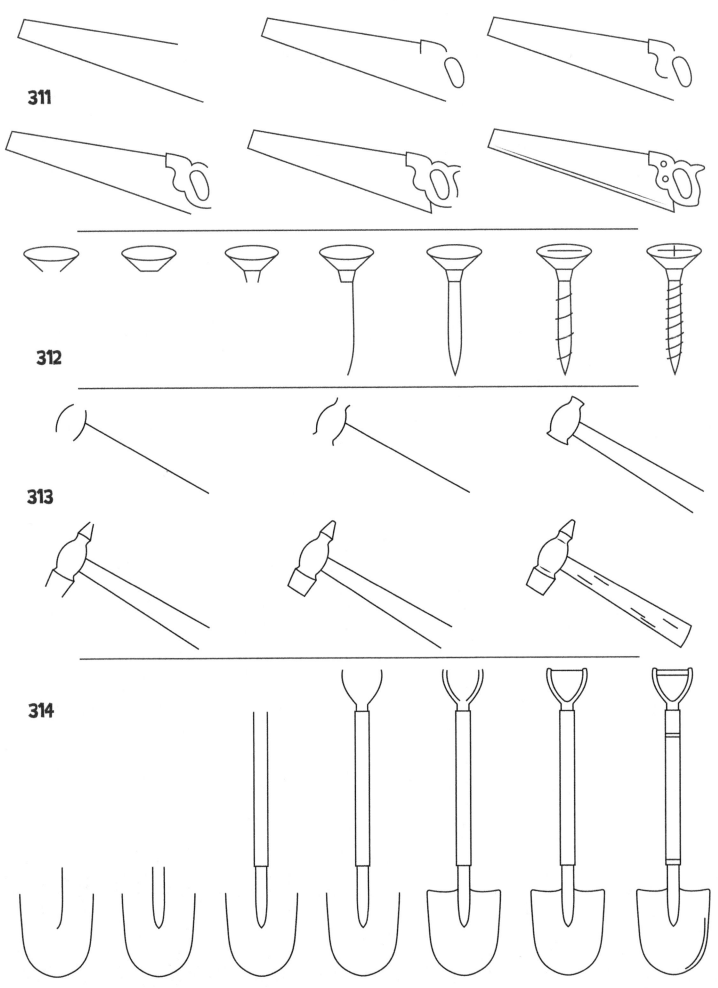

311

312

313

314

315

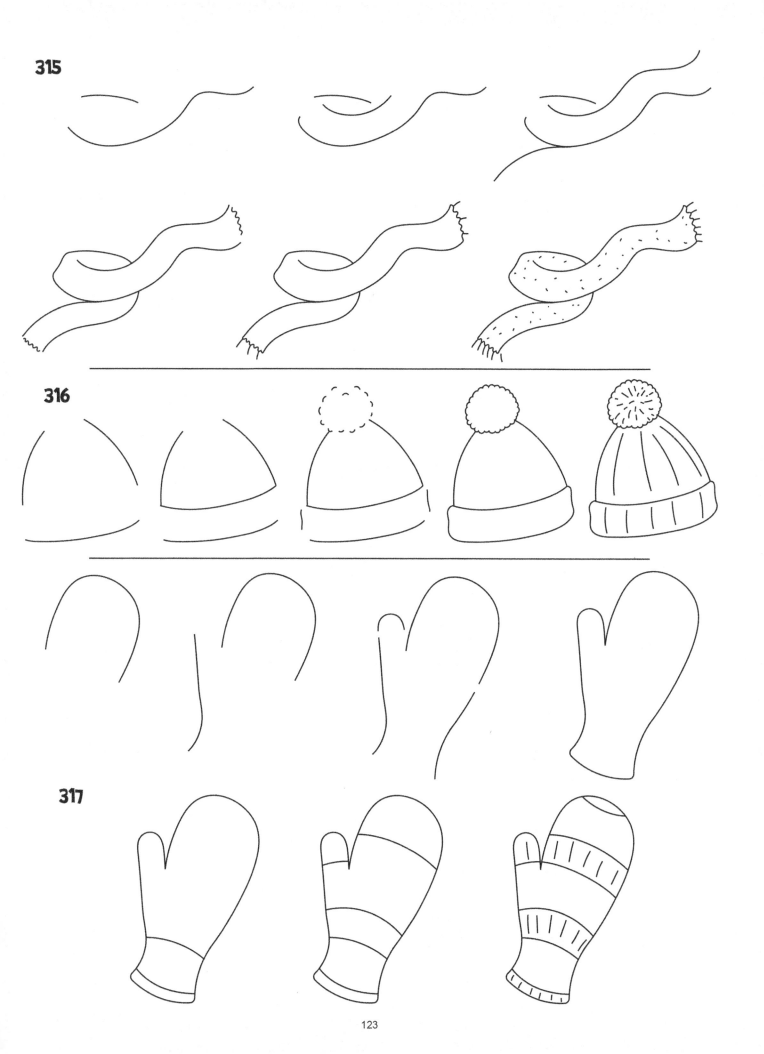

316

317

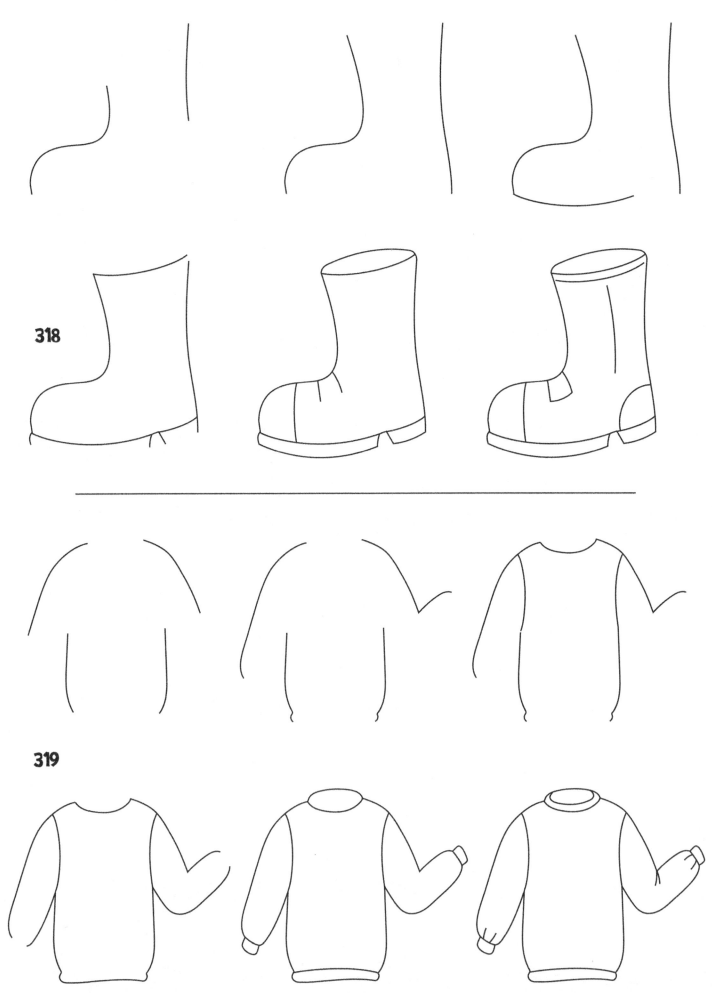

318

319

320

321

322

323

324

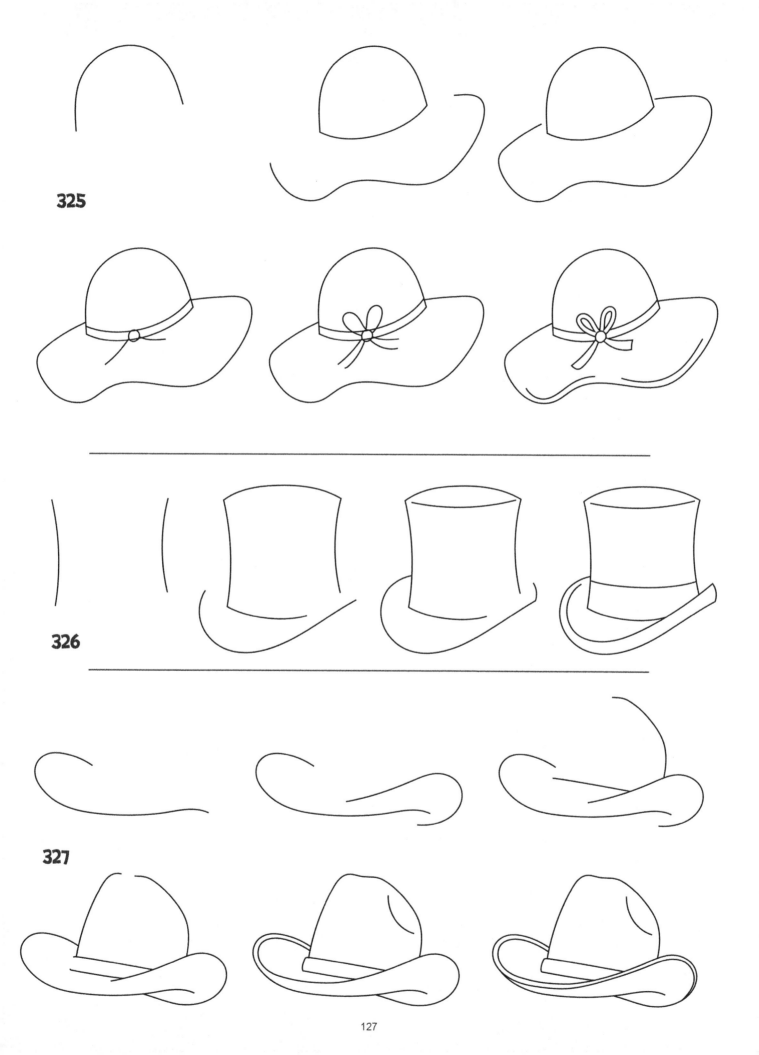

325

326

327

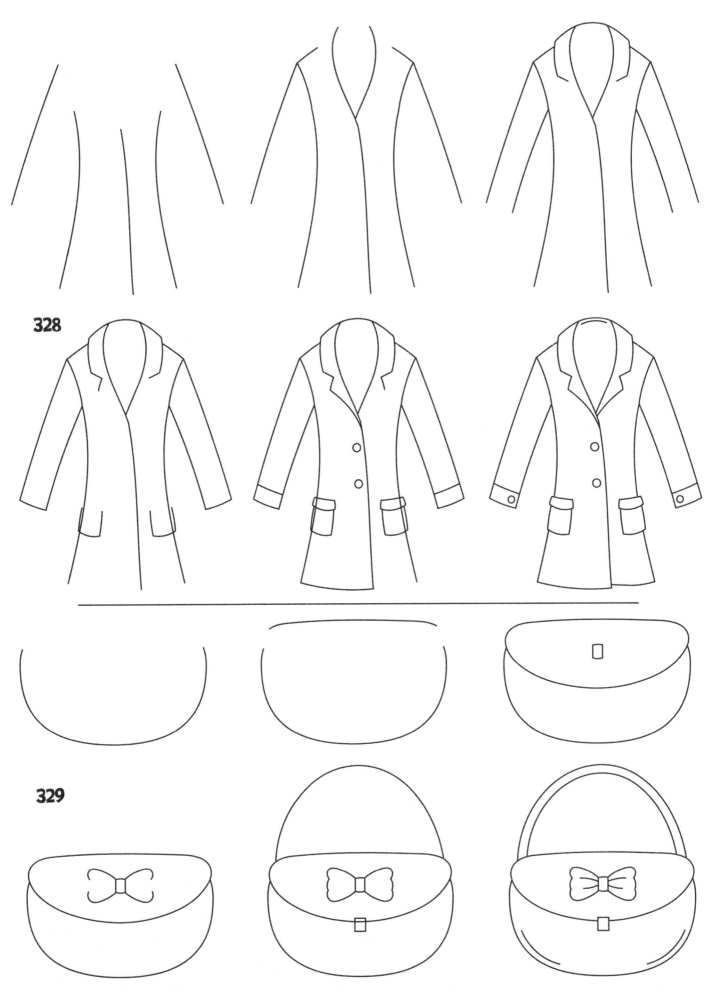

328

329

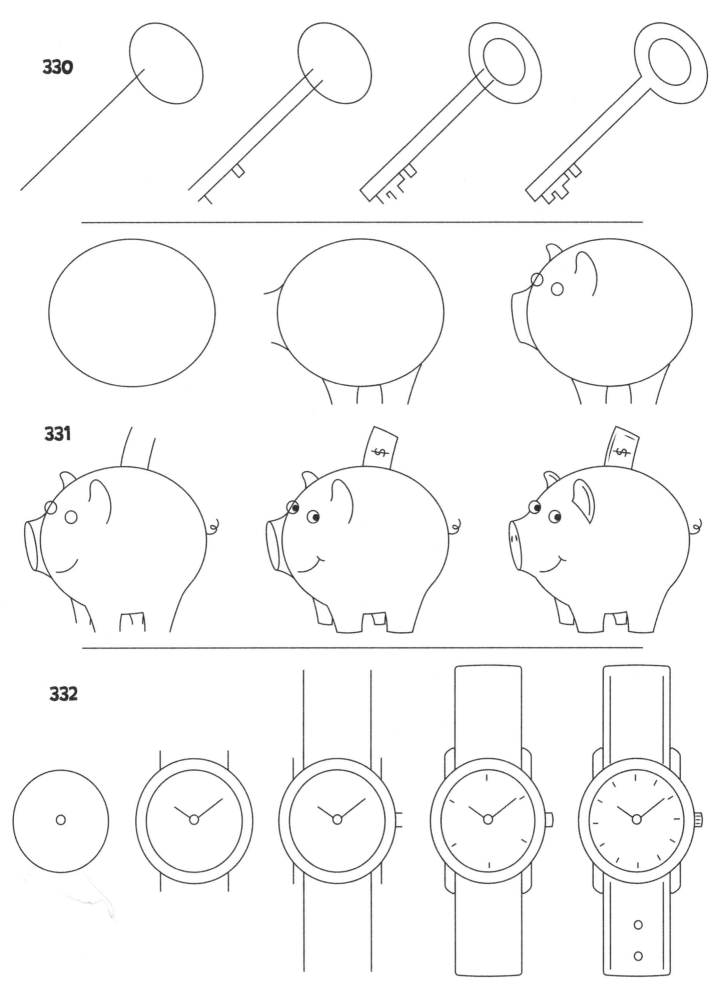

330

331

332

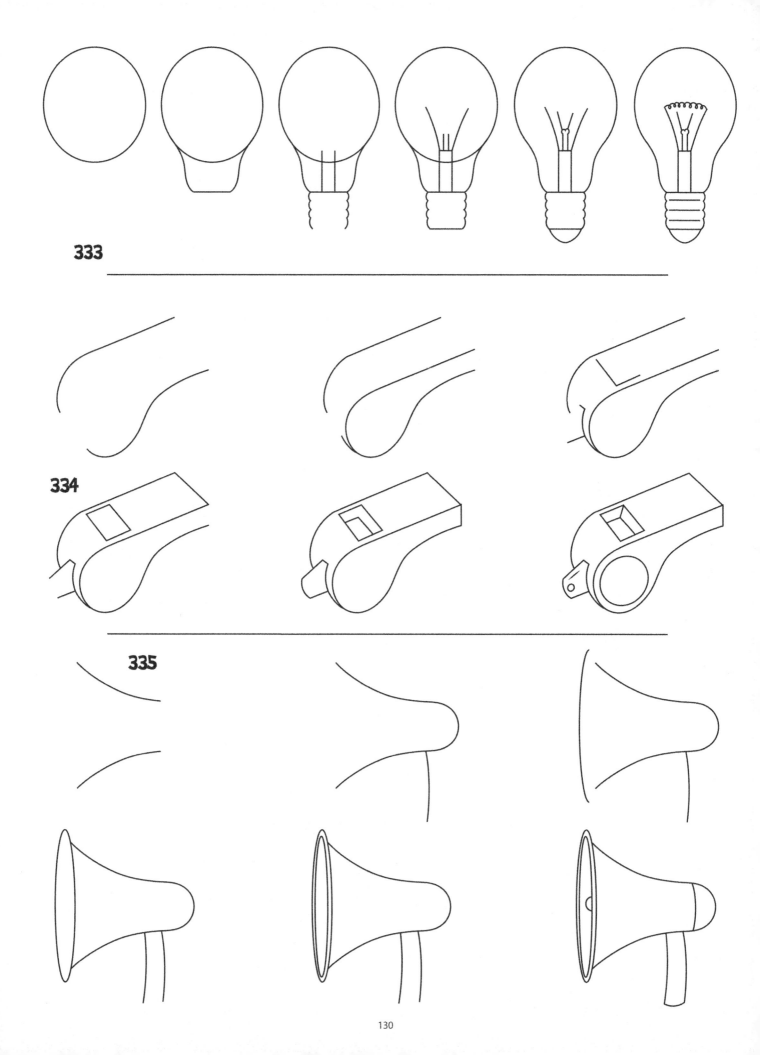

333

334

335

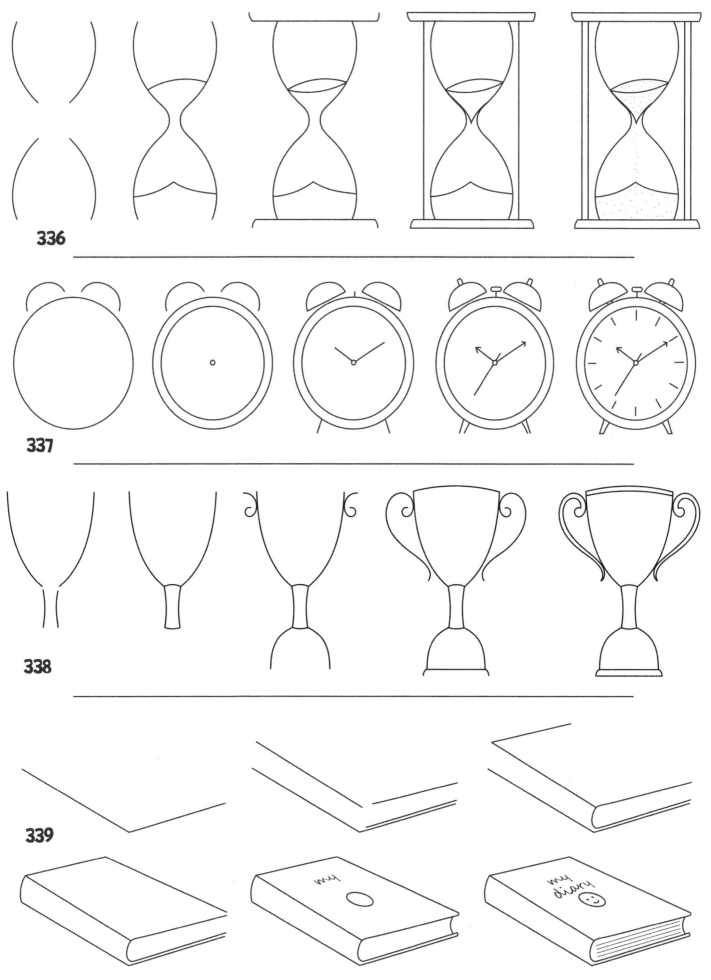

336

337

338

339

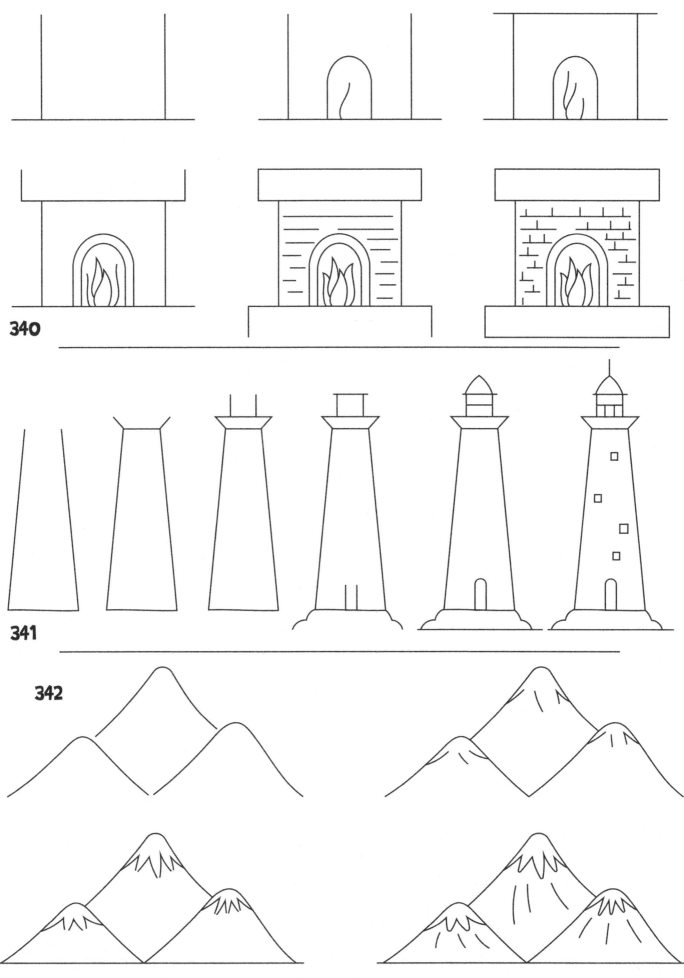

340

341

342

343

344

345

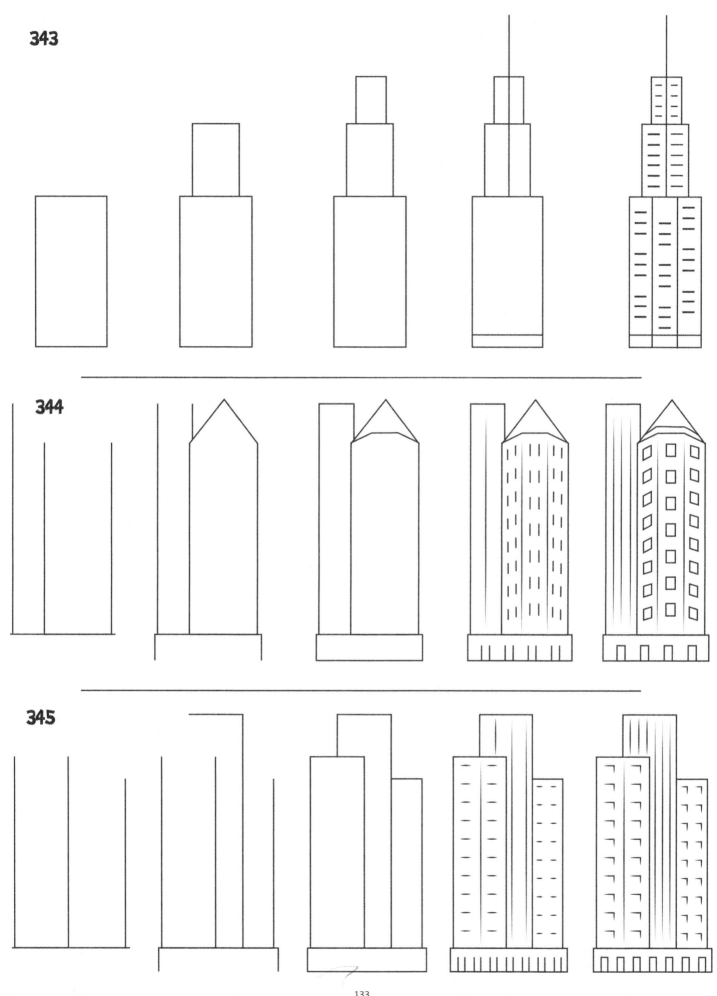

346

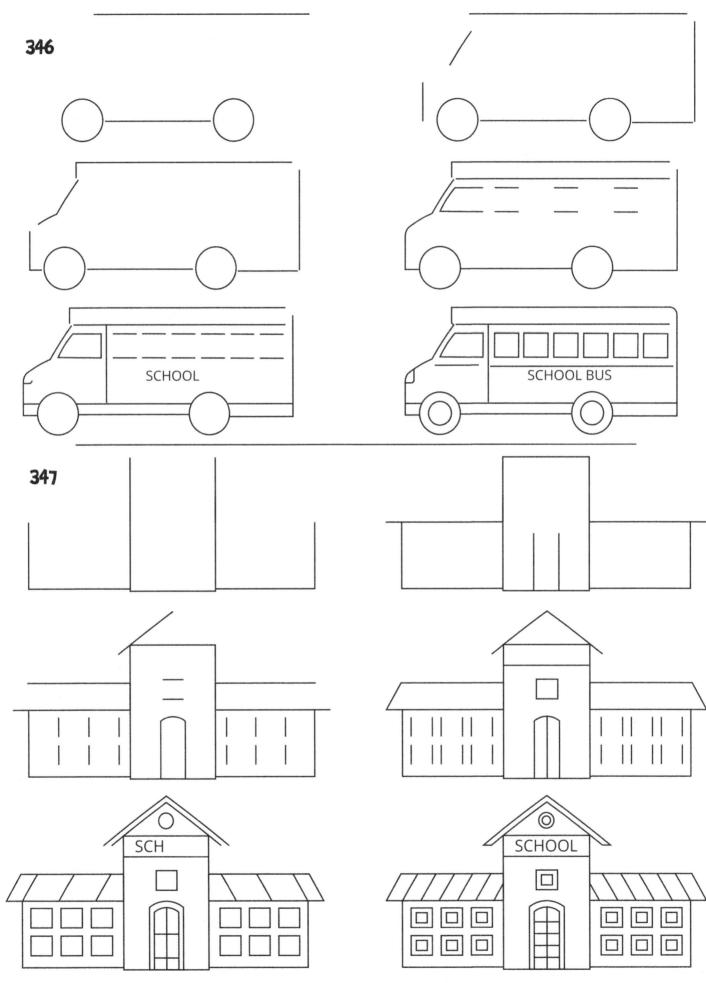

SCHOOL

SCHOOL BUS

347

SCH

SCHOOL

348

349

350

351

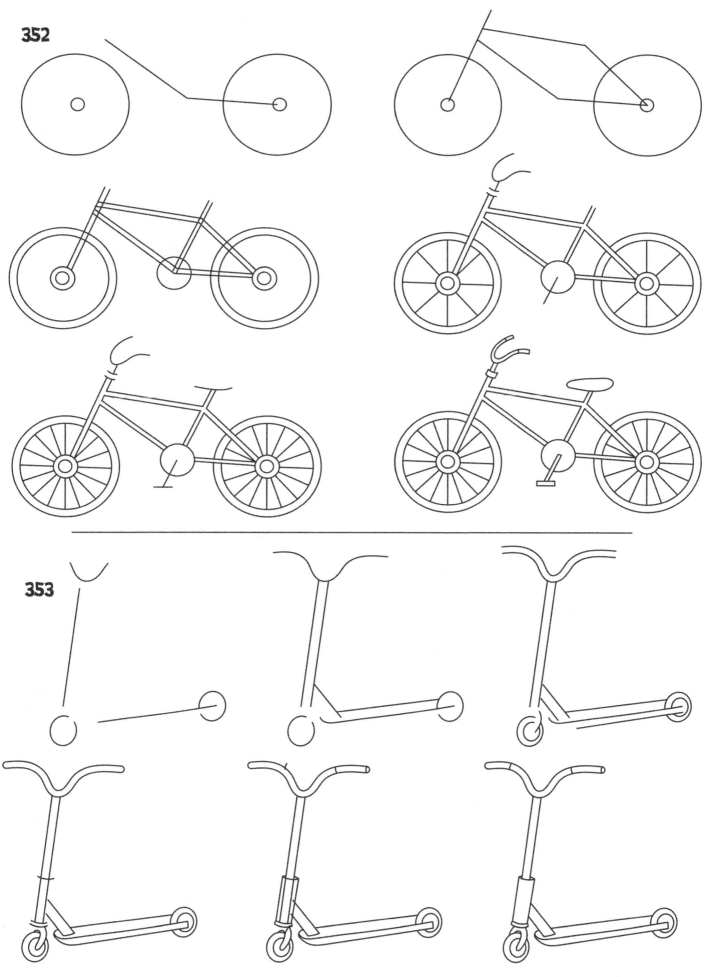

352

353

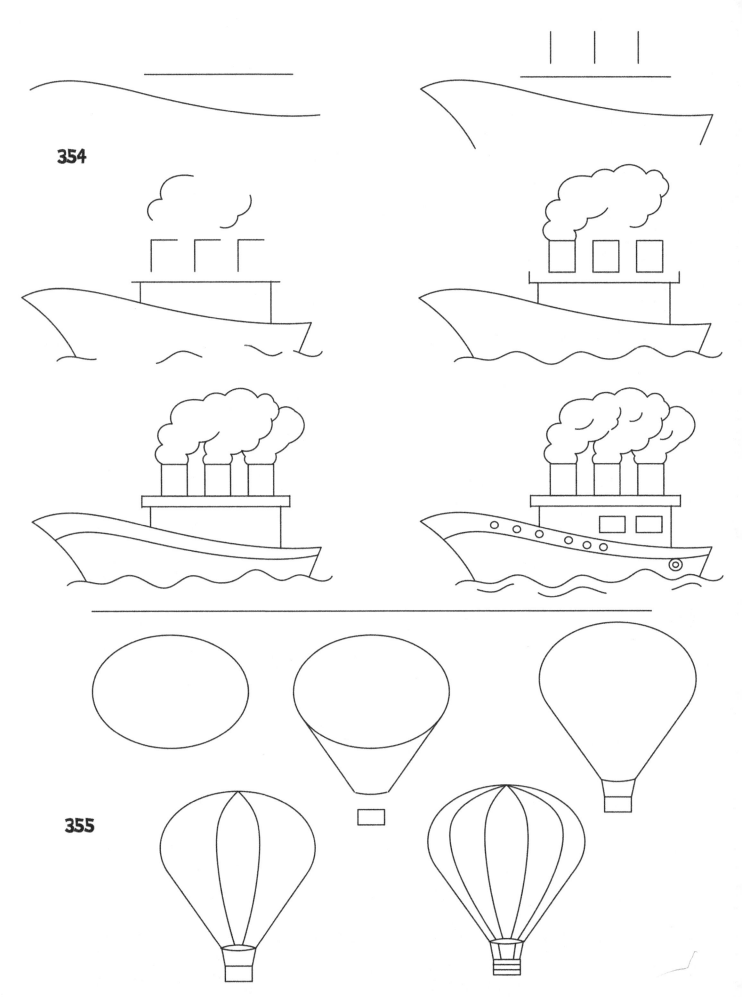

354

355

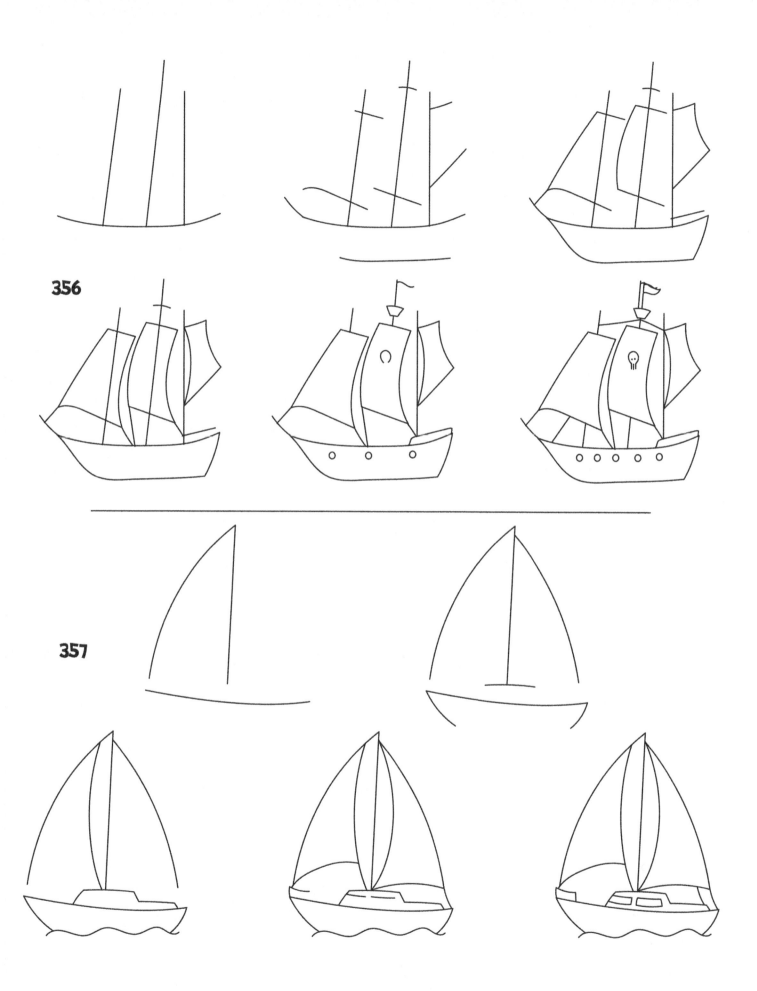

356

357

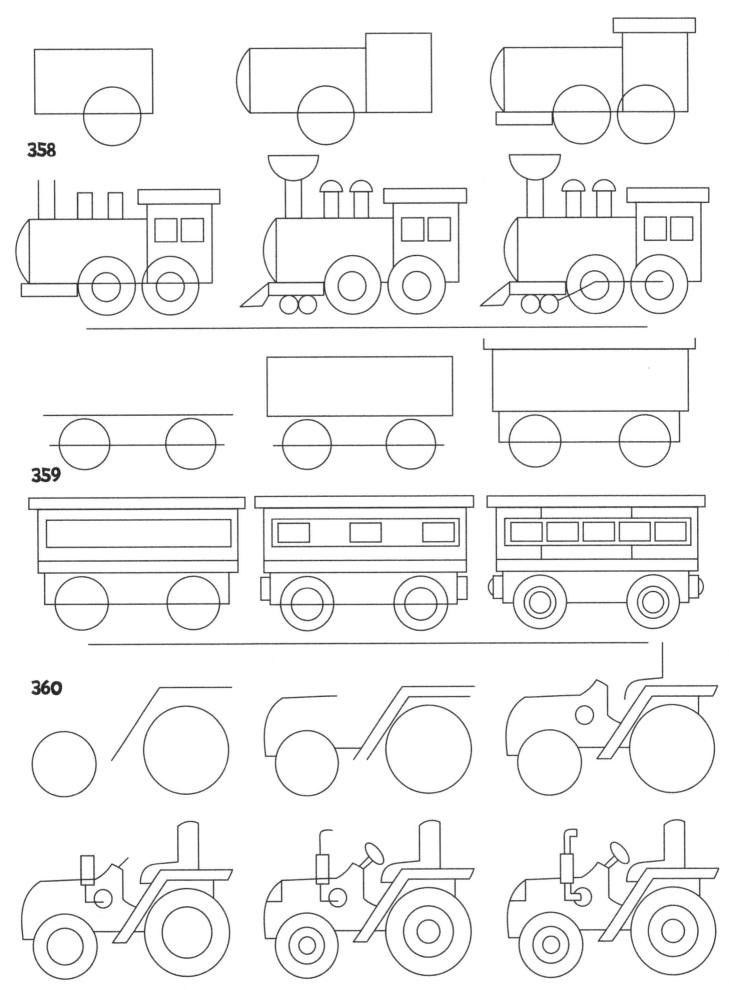

358

359

360

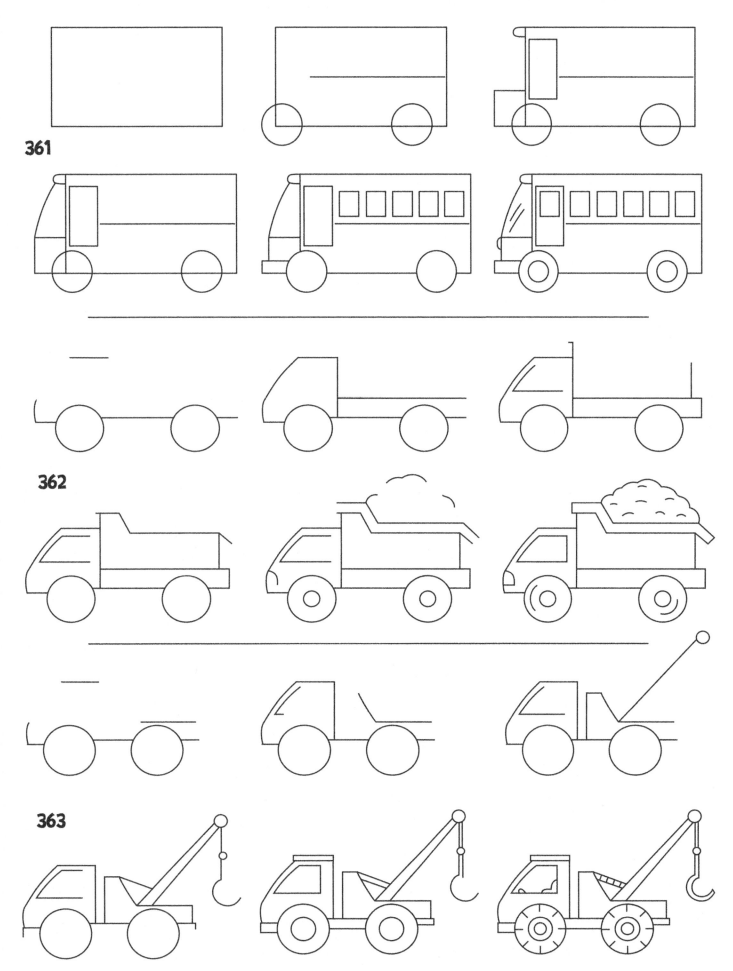

361

362

363

364

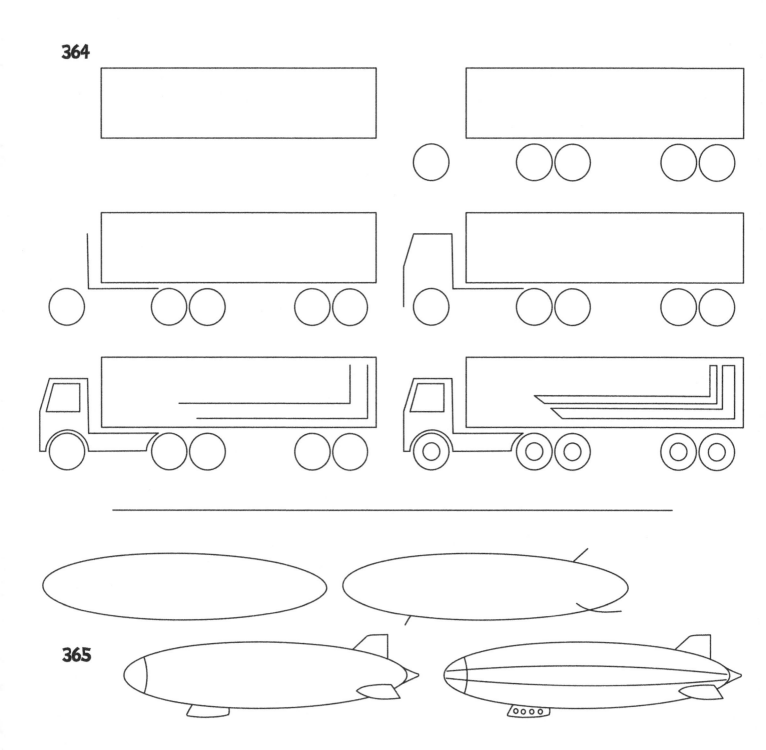

365

Free DOWNLOAD!

Like this book?

Join our VIP mailing list and get a _FREE_ 70 page printable PDF _Holiday Activity Book for Kids_! It includes crosswords, word searches, picture matching, and coloring activities for ages 4-10!

Holidays include:
  Martin Luther King Jr. Day
  Valentine's Day
  St. Patrick's Day
  Easter
  Earth Day
  4th of July
  Halloween
  Thanksgiving
  Hanukkah
  Christmas

Get started here:

www.woojr.com/VIP